Cleopatra

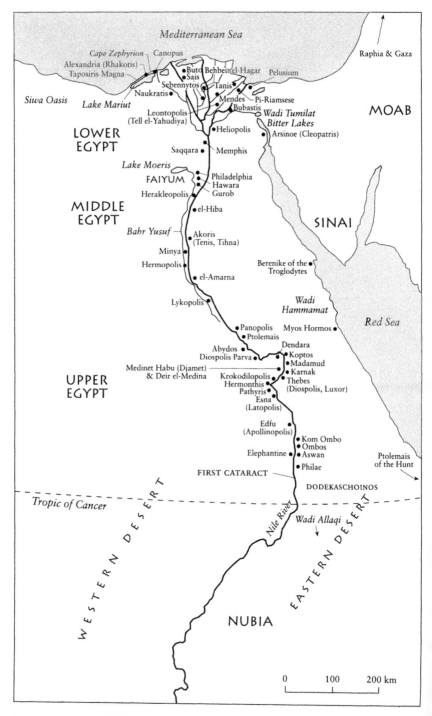

Egypt in the time of Cleopatra

CLEOPATRA

Beyond the Myth

MICHEL CHAUVEAU

translated from the French by David Lorton

Cornell University Press

Ithaca and London

Original French edition, *Cleopâtre au-delà du mythe*, copyright © 1998 by Éditions Liana Levi, Paris

English translation copyright © 2002 by Cornell University

First published 2002 by Cornell University Press
First printing, Cornell paperbacks, 2004

Library of Congress Cataloging-in-Publication Data

Chauveau, Michel.
  [Cleopatre. English]
  Cleopatra : beyond the myth / by Michel Chauveau ; translated from the French by David Lorton.
    p. cm.
  Includes bibliographical references and index.
ISBN 978-0-80143-867-7

  1. Cleopatra, Queen of Egypt, d. 30 B.C. 2.
Queens—Egypt—Biography.   I. Title.
  DT97.2.C4713 2002
  932'.021—dc21   2001004722

Cloth printing   10 9 8 7 6 5 4 3 2 1
Paperback printing   10 9 8 7 6 5 4 3 2 1

Contents

Contents

Translator's Note

English-speaking Egyptologists have no single set of conventions for the rendering of ancient Egyptian and modern Arabic personal and place names. Most of the names mentioned in this book occur in a standard reference work, John Baines and Jaromír Málek, *Atlas of Ancient Egypt* (New York, 1980), and the renderings here follow that volume. The only exception is the omission of the typographical sign for *ayin;* this consonant does not exist in English, and it was felt that its inclusion would only distract the reader.

There is also no single set of conventions for transliterating ancient Greek words and names into the Roman alphabet. The system followed here is essentially that used by Dorothy J. Thomson in *Memphis under the Ptolemies* (Princeton, 1988), the principal exception being the name of Cleopatra herself, for which the more familiar spelling has been retained here.

"It is a challenge to separate fact from rumor and legend," writes Michel Chauveau of Cleopatra, and it is difficult to imagine an Egyptologist and Hellenist better equipped than he to meet the challenge of discovering the real woman behind the myth. I wish to thank Cornell University Press for inviting me to translate this delightful volume about one of the most famous, yet also one of the most elusive, figures in history.

D.L.

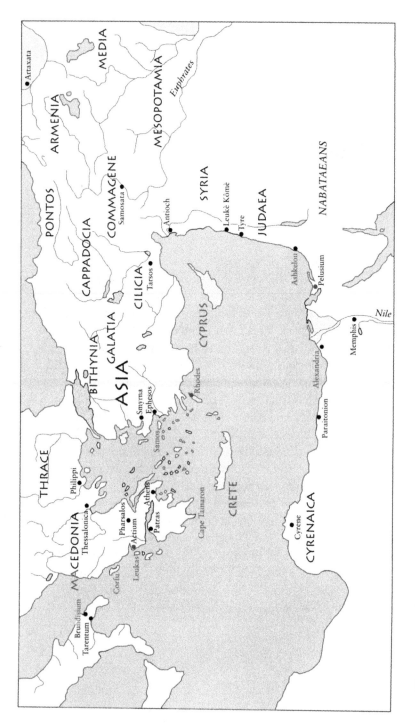

The eastern Mediterranean in the time of Cleopatra

Cleopatra

Introduction: A Personage and Her Myth

In the history of our Western world, few figures have left as distinctive a mark on the collective imagination as the last queen of ancient Egypt. In fact, Cleopatra was one of the few women who have been a dominant factor in the political events of their times. Furthermore, since fortune had it that Rome's imperial regime was born from her defeat, Cleopatra played the role, as unique as it was involuntary, of link between the Hellenistic and the Roman worlds. But that alone does not explain the singular fascination she has continuously exerted from antiquity to our own day. This fascination renews itself with every change in literary and artistic preoccupation, whether the subject is treated as an ethical commonplace or as a fantastical symbol.

Although the biographies of Cleopatra written since the nineteenth century—some aiming at objectivity and some to one degree or another fictional—have been numerous, they have apparently not exhausted the public interest. But this profusion conceals a gap: We do not in fact have any ancient account of her reign, not even a simple biographical summary! To be sure, she appears frequently in Greek and Latin accounts from the last four centuries of antiquity, but these are mere mentions that never constitute the principal focus of the works.

Such a situation is far from rare in classical historiography: only a tiny portion of the works of the ancient historians, biographers, and annalists has survived to our day, that portion which the epitomizers, the compilers, and the scribal workshops of late classical antiquity deigned to transmit to us. This is why entire areas of ancient history have fallen into oblivion. Such selectivity was not, however, a matter of chance. The center always had precedence over the periphery: for example, the internal affairs of Rome are treated at length, while the history of the states conquered by Rome are reported only from the perspective of their defeat. For its part, Christian apologetics contributed to the choice of the authors and texts that were preserved. The necessity of having a historical counterpoint to the books of the New Testament led to the preservation of the works of Flavius Josephus, a Jewish historian allied with the Romans, a circumstance that renders us better informed about the affairs of Palestine at the time of Christ than about those of the rest of the Mediterranean world, with the exception of Rome.

From the purely historical point of view, Cleopatra is thus but an empty figure without an existence of her own, the privileged but ever subordinate partner in the lives of her contemporaries: Julius Caesar, Mark Antony, Octavian, and even Herod, king of the Jews. Still, the evocative richness of the rare anecdotes concerning her have gone far to compensate for the lack of a continuous narrative, even shedding a particular light on her person that a fuller integration into the thread of history would inevitably have dimmed, a fact that partly explains the popularity she has enjoyed with posterity.

Recounting the life of Cleopatra always entails the risk of saying more about her contemporaries than about her, more about Rome or Asia Minor than about Egypt, more about her dreams than about the real person. These pitfalls are difficult to avoid: What would Cleopatra have been without Caesar and Antony at a time when Egypt was scarcely more than a satellite of Rome?

An account of the queen's personality would not suffice to explain her exceptional destiny, which cannot be separated from its historical and cultural context. Moreover, even before her life was over, she had already been swallowed up in her myth. The origin and development of this myth are incredibly complex, and history alone cannot furnish all the keys to it. We shall therefore attempt to exorcise the myth and to reduce the person of Cleopatra to the facts—that is, to what the ancient writers reported and to what we learn from contemporary documents. Since the former abound in contradictions and improbabilities, and the latter have often been the object of risky or even contradictory interpretations, readers will understand that this apparently modest goal could easily constitute a foolhardy enterprise. They will therefore more easily pardon the limits of this modest work, which will have achieved its aim if it does nothing more than undermine the certitudes and clichés that have been spread by an abundant but too often complaisant literature.

N.B.: Except where otherwise noted, all dates herein are B.C.E.

"A Queen Issued from
So Many Kings"

The Heritage

The reign of Cleopatra represented the end of one of humanity's greatest adventures, which began with Alexander's conquest
of the East, from the Nile to the Indus, permitting the formation
of states with mixed, multicultural populations dominated by a
Greek or Hellenized minority. These states experienced diverse
fortunes during the three centuries that followed the death of
Alexander in 323, as they wore themselves out in struggles for an
unattainable hegemony. Rome, which had been growing into a
great power since the end of the third century, profited from
these struggles by gradually imposing its own rule on them. By
the middle of the first century, scarcely any of these kingdoms
remained besides Egypt, the only one whose continued survival
Rome had tolerated.

Cleopatra's family, the Lagides, established itself in Egypt in
323 in the person of Ptolemy, son of Lagos, one of Alexander's
Macedonian companions. Ptolemy and his immediate successors
dominated all of the eastern Mediterranean and made Alexandria,
their capital, the largest, richest, and most prestigious city of their
time. From the beginning of the dynasty on, their queens assumed an eminent political and ideological role, in particular

4

when Ptolemy II married his sister Arsinoe II around 274. In doing so, he established a precedent for the incestuous marriages of a number of his descendants and guaranteed the quasi-divine essence of the royal family.

The seventh Cleopatra was thus heir to a line of determined women who were often the object of sincere devotion on the part of the Egyptian people and who did not hesitate to exercise effective power in the place of inept or discredited husbands or sons. Though the Arsinoes, the Berenikes, and the early Cleopatras have not enjoyed the fame of their last descendant, this is certainly not for lack of character or political genius, but for lack of partners or adversaries of the stature of a Caesar or an Antony. In any case, these queens had little responsibility for the crises that befell the Lagide state and led to its decline during the century and a half that preceded the birth of Cleopatra VII.

In fact, the situation in the Ptolemaic kingdom by around the year 50 was dismal. Again, we must make a distinction between the condition of Egypt itself and that of its capital. Egypt remained a singularly rich land whose primarily agricultural wealth had enabled it to nourish a huge population since remote antiquity. The land also had a long tradition of economic and administrative organization that tended toward self-sufficiency. The Ptolemaic monarchy was poured into this already highly structured mold, to which it added the concept of profit, along with the general use of coinage and the introduction of a banking system. The king headed a veritable business enterprise that extended throughout the land. State monopolies and taxes weighed upon all stages of production and exchange, all of it administered by a bloated and strictly hierarchized bureaucracy that implemented a superabundance of nit-picking regulations. We can easily understand how the revenues enjoyed by the Lagide crown, thanks to this gigantic system of exploitation, attracted the greedy instincts of certain parties in Rome. Nevertheless, these apparent riches concealed the dramatic misery of the countryside, where the most visible signs were the desertion of villages and a lack of security even in the temples.[1]

Alexandria, Rival of Rome

History knows few examples in which the destiny of a capital was so dissociated from that of its land. The founding of Alexandria in 331 on the Mediterranean coast of Egypt offered the country the coastal port it had always lacked. Via Alexandria, Egyptian products could easily be exported to the East, as well as to Greece and Italy. But Alexandria was a Greek city, the only one founded in Egypt besides the old colony of Naukratis, which was stagnating, and the more recent Ptolemaïs in the Thebais. Alexandria was so distant from the venerable native centers that the Egyptians never recognized it as their true capital. It was all the more foreign in that its civic body was composed exclusively of Greeks. In fact, a highly mixed population was crowded into the wide streets of the city: In addition to descendants of the original Greek and Macedonian colonists, there were many more or less Hellenized immigrants from throughout the East, many of them Jews—and, to be sure, some Egyptians, who could not be excluded indefinitely. More than two and a half centuries after it was founded, Alexandria was undoubtedly the largest city in the world, though Rome was already in a position to dispute that title. Still, Alexandria's star had perceptibly dimmed since the time of the Philadelphoi and the Euergetai, when it could lay claim to being the cultural capital of the Hellenistic world. The scholars and artists of the Museum had allowed their power to become entangled in the dynastic struggles, which led to their expulsion under King Ptolemy VIII, Cleopatra's great-grandfather. At a stroke the intellectual life was drained from a city that would from that time on be uniquely perturbed by the moods of its headstrong population. Happily, some sixty years later, a reverse flow of scholars restored some color to Alexandrian culture, when an implacable war declared by Mithridates of Pontos against the Romans and their allies ravaged Asia Minor and threatened Greece. With Alexandria the only secure place in the East, intellectuals suddenly flocked there to seek refuge with the king of Egypt, who was thrilled to regain his prestige.

In any event, Alexandria and Egypt were the remaining jewels in the Lagide crown. Nothing was left of the maritime empire of the early Ptolemies. Of its two last foreign possessions, Cyrenaica and Cyprus, the first had been ceded to the Romans by its last ruler, an illegitimate son of Ptolemy VIII. One of Cleopatra's uncles, an obscure Ptolemy, still ruled the second. The rest of the Mediterranean basin was subject to Rome. But not all the East was directly administered by the latter. The Roman provinces were still few in number, and they occupied a rather limited expanse of territory. The disappearance of the great empires had in fact led to a proliferation of tiny kingdoms and city-states that were frequently united in loose confederations, all of them "friends and allies of the Senate and the Roman People" and all of them vassals of Rome. Larger nations—less Hellenized and mostly hostile—bordering on the homogeneous coastal strip of the Mediterranean lay in wait for any opportunity to wrest direct access to that sea: the kingdom of Pontos on the shores of the Black Sea; Armenia, bordering the foothills of the Caucasus; Arabia of the Nabataeans; and above all Parthia, whose rulers claimed the heritage of the earlier Achaemenids defeated by Alexander and whose territory comprised modern Iran and Iraq.

Despite the relative weakness of its dynasty, Egypt remained the second power in the Mediterranean basin after Rome; in fact, Egypt was the only land that could discommode Rome, at least on the economic level, given that Egypt possessed the last great

69—the very year to which the birth of our Cleopatra is to be assigned! We do not know whether this disappearance is due to the
death of the queen—in which case Strabo could be correct—or
whether she perhaps fell into disgrace. Some historians favoring
the latter hypothesis would have Cleopatra Tryphene reappear in
58, when Ptolemy XII fled to Rome.[4] She would then have
seized power, along with her daughter Berenike IV, before dying
a year later, leaving Berenike alone to face the return of her father. But Porphyry of Tyre, the only writer to report this
episode,[5] states that this Cleopatra, who would have reigned
from 58 to 57, was not Ptolemy XII's wife, but rather another of
this king's daughters, a Cleopatra who is otherwise unknown!
The problem thus seems insoluble.

In any case, Cleopatra's possible illegitimacy in no way influ-
enced her political fortune, and we find no allusions to it among
the innumerable attacks, both contemporary and posthumous,
that were directed against the queen. Daughter of the royal
couple, fruit of a morganatic union, or even illegitimate, Cleopatra guards the secret of her origins.

We know little more regarding her childhood and adoles-
cence. Raised with the other children in the deleterious milieu of
the palaces of Alexandria, she would undoubtedly have had qualified teachers who assured her education. It is true that the sexism
of the Hellenic tradition in the matter of pedagogy condemned
girls to near ignorance, for only boys were admitted to the *gym-
nasion* and thus to instruction. At the court of the Ptolemies, the
education of princes was placed in the hands of tutors who were
trustworthy men with distinguished minds. In the early years of
the dynasty, this essential task was entrusted to highly respected
scholars who exercised their talents in the framework of the Museum. It was thus that Ptolemy III could benefit from the lessons
of Apollonios of Rhodes, the author of the *Argonautika*.

In view of the increasing influence of the Lagide women, it is probable that the princesses also profited from the services of competent tutors. In the case of Cleopatra, the remarkable intelligence with which the ancient writers unanimously credit her was surely due to her innate ability, but the charm of her conversation and the refinement of her manners could have resulted only from a meticulous education. Yet it is difficult to credit the latter with the exceptional mastery the queen acquired of several "barbarian" languages.[6] Instruction in foreign languages was scarcely a part of Hellenic education, for the Greeks were thoroughly imbued with their own culture. In fact, none of the Ptolemies had deigned to learn the native tongue of the majority of their subjects, the Demotic stage of the Egyptian language. Cleopatra thus stands out as a veritable phenomenon in her dynasty. Some scholars have even speculated that her knowledge of Egyptian could be explained by the supposed origin of her mother, who, if she was not Cleopatra Tryphene, could in fact have belonged to the family of the high priests of Memphis.[7] The exponents of this hypothesis, which relies on the flimsiest of evidence, cannot employ it to explain how the queen was also able to learn Hebrew, Aramaic, Arabic, Ethiopian, Median, Parthian, Latin, which she could scarcely ignore, and even the language of the troglodytes. She had an incontestable gift for languages and an uncommonly curious and open mind. The other side of her education stemmed from her experience observing the mores of the royal court and the political intrigues that marked the end of her father's reign.

The New Dionysos

Hoisted abruptly to the throne by a tragedy in the palace, Ptolemy XII (Figure 1) was a mere bastard ill-prepared to confront the pitfalls of power. It did him little good to assume the

Figure 1. Marble statue head depicting Ptolemy XII Auletes. The Louvre. Photo by H. Lewandowski, courtesy of Réunion des Musées Nationaux/Art Resource, New York.

epithets Philopator ("who loves his father") and Philadelphos ("who loves his brother/sister") to perpetuate the mystique of the dynasty, for the fear engendered in him by his sudden fortune informed all his conduct as king. For this reason, he went further than any of his ancestors in promoting his personal cult by proclaiming himself the "God New Dionysos," a pretense that in fact earned him the ridiculing sobriquet "flute player" (Auletes). Conscious that he owed his elevation to nothing more than the capricious will of an urban mob run amok, he searched feverishly for an external support on which he could base his dubious legitimacy.

He could find such support only in the might of Rome. There, certain interest groups were dreaming of annexing Egypt, all the more so given that they had a legal argument for laying claim to it. In 88, an uncle of Ptolemy XII, Ptolemy Alexander, had willed the kingdom of Egypt to the Senate and the Roman People as a last resort to block the return of his brother Ptolemy IX. At the time, no one in Rome had envisaged claiming such an inheritance, for everyone was obsessed with the civil war that was raging and with the threat posed by Mithridates. In 80, the latter was at bay, and Sulla was sole master of Rome. Conditions were ripe for the appearance in Alexandria of a new king of dubious legitimacy to arouse a sudden interest in the testament of Ptolemy Alexander. Over the years, the question of Egypt had become a recurrent subject in Roman political debate. Some went so far as to imagine turning Egypt into a housing project for the Roman poor! Cicero and others vigorously opposed such extreme schemes, for they saw in them the risk of the emergence of a new tyranny.[8]

For his part, Ptolemy XII also strove to defeat such schemes, heaping his largess on anyone who might contribute to his official recognition. His extravagant efforts were finally rewarded in 59: Caesar, who was consul for the year, and the great Pompey himself, royally rewarded for this service, persuaded the senators to award him the title of "friend and ally of the Roman People." But to satisfy the desires of the partisans of annexation, the Popular Assembly decided instead to take possession of Cyprus. The passiveness with which Ptolemy accepted this seizure of his brother's realm outraged the people of Alexandria, who rose up in revolt in 58.

The king precipitously fled the city to take refuge with his new allies, leaving the power perhaps in the hands of his wife, but more likely in those of his oldest daughter, Berenike. After various attempts that failed because of political complexities in Rome, Auletes succeeded in buying the governor of the province of Syria, Aulus Gabinius, who reestablished him on his throne by force of arms in the spring of 55.

Cleopatra witnessed the atrocities that accompanied her father's return to Alexandria: the murder of her older sister and the latter's friends; the excesses of Gabinius's legionaries, many of them soldiers of Germanic and Gallic origin, in a city that had never known a foreign occupation; and the reign of terror that descended upon all those who did not manifest sufficient enthusiasm for the restoration of the New Dionysos. In light of her future conduct, we can imagine the nature of the lessons that she learned from these terrible events: to eliminate as quickly as possible every potential rival within her own family, to ally herself with a Roman military force that she could not succeed in confronting, and to make herself popular by all possible means. Moreover, she did not hesitate to display the precocious political maturity that such an experience had developed in her.

One of her father's last political acts was to rid himself of the Roman financier Rabirius Postumus, whose loans had enabled him to regain his throne. He appointed Postumus as *dioiketes*— that is, minister of finances—so that he could reimburse himself for Ptolemy's debts by drawing directly on the source of the king's revenues, the tax payments of the Egyptian people. Ill informed regarding the customs of the land, the rapacious banker aroused such discontent that only flight saved him from the fury of an unbridled mob. Shortly after this gratifying episode, the king fell gravely ill, making the problem of his succession a critical one.

A Perilous Succession

The history of the dynasty had shown that dissension among the heirs constituted the greatest danger to the peace and unity of the land. After eliminating Berenike, his oldest daughter, Ptolemy XII still had four children, two of whom were girls. He attempted to prevent family quarrels by means of the bond of the dynastic cult, uniting all his issue in a college of the "New Gods Philadelphos."[9] In doing so, he invoked the virtues of the brotherly love that, in the glorious days of his ancestors Ptolemy II and Arsinoe Philadelphos, had assured the prosperity of Egypt and the future of the dynasty. He must have been attempting to establish a sort of joint rule, a solution that had precedents but which had in practice proved to be fragile.

From the slightest of indications, we can discern the schemes that were hatched around the declining king to impose some other arrangement for the succession. The royal court at Alexandria had always been torn between various cliques that competed for government titles and positions. Given the prospect of such an uncertain change of reign, each of these factions tried to maneuver itself into the most advantageous position possible. The testament that the king ultimately decided to place in the hands of the Roman senate to guarantee its execution provided for a shared regency between Ptolemy XIII, the older of the boys, and Cleopatra, the older girl. The senate entrusted the testament to Pompey, at that time the master of Rome, who regarded himself as the unofficial protector of the Lagides—but would that suffice to assure that the testament would be respected?

The events that followed are so obscure that the question seems impossible to answer; even the date of Ptolemy XII's death is unknown. This uncertainty was shared by contemporaries; in Rome, the news was for a long time only a rumor, confirmed around the thirtieth of June.[10] For some months, in fact—from May to July 51—official documents were jointly dated to year 30 (of Auletes) and year 1 (of the new reign). To account for such an unusual step, we must imagine that the aged king, who was undoubtedly on his deathbed, was incapable of ruling, and that the elevation of his successor was thus being anticipated. We can thus suppose that none had profited from this delay so as to reorganize the inheritance to his or her own convenience by ignoring the provisions of the testament.

Cleopatra could have been the beneficiary of such maneuvers. According to a well-known hieroglyphic stela[11] set up in the first regnal year of Augustus, the queen would have participated, on her own initiative, in the enthronement of the sacred Buchis bull in the Theban region on March 22, 51. Nevertheless, a critical examination of the text does not enable us to confirm an actual royal presence at this native religious festival. Incidentally, Cleopatra's independent position vis-à-vis her brother has also been deduced from an anecdote related by Valerius Maximus, a Roman moralist who was active during the reign of the emperor Tiberius (14–37 C.E.). According to this writer,[12] Cleopatra alone took the initiative of arresting and extraditing the assassins of the two sons of the governor of Syria, Calpurnius Bibulus, who was in office in 51–50. The two young men had been murdered while on a mission to Egypt to bring back the soldiers left behind by Gabinius some years earlier. If Cleopatra could thus act in her own name, are we to conclude that she had already displaced her brother from the throne?

The matter is not that simple: Rather, several generations after Cleopatra, a Latin writer likely remembered only her name, which had become famous, while her brother-husband had fallen into oblivion. There are also two documents written in Greek, a stela[13] and a papyrus,[14] that are dated to the first year of Cleopatra, the "goddess Philopator," with no mention of her possible coregent. Some scholars have thought that the Cleopatra cited in these texts is indeed Cleopatra VII. Nothing, however, prevents us from taking her to be Cleopatra-Berenike III, daughter of Ptolemy IX, who ruled for a scant six months after the death of her father and who also had the epithet "goddess Philopator." The two texts in question could thus be dated to the summer of the year 80 rather than to the summer of 51, where their modern editors might have situated them too hastily.

The events that surrounded and followed the death of Ptolemy XII thus remain an enigma. As frustrating as it may seem, it is nearly impossible to verify Cleopatra's activities during the troubled period that preceded the successive arrivals of the two ex-triumvirs Pompey and Caesar in Egypt in the fall of 48. The classical authors, interested only in the Roman point of view, mention events in Egypt only when the latter could have interfered with the affairs of Rome. This is certainly the case with the assassination of the sons of the governor of Syria. Unfortunately, this isolated sad fact teaches us almost nothing about the internal situation of Egypt beyond the constant threat posed by the soldiers whom Gabinius had abandoned to their fate.

In the same manner, Appian and Plutarch mentioned the visit to Alexandria by another noted figure, Gnaeus Pompey the younger, the son of Pompey the Great.[15] The latter had just fled Italy before the advance of Caesar, who had declared war by crossing the Rubicon on December 17, 50.[16] The younger Pompey's mission was to ask the Ptolemaic government for men, provisions, and vessels as a contribution to the war against Caesar. He succeeded in obtaining sixty ships, plus five hundred veterans from Gabinius's army, who agreed to follow him, and a large quantity of wheat destined for Dyrrhachium, where his father had retreated. Despite Appian's assertion regarding Cleopatra's preeminence, this agreement was apparently concluded in the name of young Ptolemy XIII, with his sister's name placed second. In fact, a papyrus in Berlin[17] preserves the text of a decree, dated to October 27, 50, that was promulgated in the names "of the king and the queen," proving that at that date, at least, Cleopatra ranked second.

The provisions of the latter decree reveal much about the situation at that time: Shipowners and merchants were forbidden to transport grain from Middle Egypt to any place but Alexandria. Those who did not comply were subject to the death penalty. Only the threat of famine could have justified such a drastic measure; unfortunately, the reason for this threat escapes us. Was it due to an act of nature, such as a low Nile inundation? Or was the political and social situation troubled to the point of interrupting the provisioning of the capital? A series of crises likely had been occurring for at least a dozen years; their causes would have been as much structural as short-term, with the political quarrels at Alexandria playing only a relatively minor role in their development. All the woes that had taken root in the Ptolemaic government's exploitation of Egypt were now reaching their climax. These included an arbitrary taxation system in which the demands were inversely proportional to a decrease in revenues, widespread corruption of royal officials, the depopulation of rural communities due to the flight of peasants overwhelmed by taxes and tax farmers, and socio-ethnic tensions between Egyptian peasants and descendants of Greek military colonists.

The Fratricidal Conflict

At the beginning of the year 49, in any case, the situation at court, as seen from the countryside of Egypt, had not yet changed. On March 15, 49, two private contracts written in Demotic continued to recognize "King Ptolemy and Queen Cleopatra, the gods who love their father" as sovereigns.[18] Toward the end of October, the Roman senate, which had sided with Pompey and was therefore in session at Thessalonica in Macedonia, officially bestowed the title of "friend and ally of the Roman People" on Ptolemy XIII in return for his assistance. Moreover, the young king was placed under Pompey's tutelage. The senate's decree made no mention of Cleopatra. What, then, had happened? The only indication we have is the enigmatic appearance at this time of a new era of dating, in which the first year (the only one attested) corresponded to year 3 of the previous era, which theoretically covered the period from September 5, 50, to September 3, 49.[19] Though none of the three papyri dated to the new era indicates the month or the day, one mentions "Queen Cleopatra and [. . .]."[20] We may thus suppose that this new manner of counting the years expressed Cleopatra's rebellion against her brother Ptolemy XIII and the coterie of courtiers who chaperoned the latter. Eighty years earlier, one of our queen's forebears, Cleopatra II, had acted likewise against her husband, Ptolemy VIII (nicknamed "Fatty"), by inaugurating a new regnal era that also proved to be ephemeral. Like her great-great-grandmother, our Cleopatra quickly lost the contest, undoubtedly before September of 49, which would explain the omission of her name in the decree of the senate at Thessalonica the following month.

To understand the sequence of events, we must cite Julius Caesar's description of the situation when his adversary Pompey arrived on the Egyptian coast on July 25, 48: "It happened that the boy-king Ptolemy was at Pelusium with a large army. He was at war with his sister Cleopatra, whom he had driven from the throne a few months earlier by the help of his relatives and friends. Cleopatra's camp was not far distant from that of Ptolemy."[21] The situation of the two Egyptian camps in the environs of Pelusium indicates that Cleopatra must have previously fled to Syria, and that in this summer of 48, she was attempting to return by force to Egypt. We have no information regarding the troops she had at her disposal. She surely had with her a circle of loyal men who had followed her into exile, but these could in no way have constituted an army capable of being led on an offensive. Her return to Egypt must thus have entailed the recruiting of mercenaries, which would have been no small matter in the context of the Roman civil war and the state of disorder the latter had created in Syria. It is possible that Cleopatra had obtained the assistance of the old Philistine city of Ashkelon, which was theoretically a free city, though it was obliged to seek allies against possible hostile attempts on the part of its Jewish and Nabataean neighbors. Curiously enough, at this time Ashkelon, which was only a six-day march from Pelusium, issued coins bearing the image of Cleopatra.[22]

Despite this assistance, the prospects of the dethroned queen were anything but bright, and this twenty-year-old's astonishing vigor was itself scarcely enough to assure the success of so audacious an operation. In fact, few armies in the past had succeeded in forcing their way past Pelusium, Egypt's defensive rampart against enemies from the east. Each time, powerful states had launched huge undertakings directed by great military leaders. Although Gabinius's legions had made their way past Pelusium without difficulty in the spring of 55, nothing more than some hastily gathered colonist-soldiers and a disorganized land stood in their way. Since the same veterans of Gabinius were now fighting at the side of Ptolemy XIII, only a stroke of luck could have saved Cleopatra.

Caesar in Egypt

It was luck indeed that suddenly intertwined the Roman civil war and the affairs of Egypt. In early June 48, Caesar (Figure 2) had achieved a decisive victory over Pompey at Pharsalos in

Figure 2. Silver denarius depicting Julius Caesar (above) and the goddess Venus Victrix. From the Ottilia Buerger Collection of Ancient and Byzantine Coins. Photo courtesy of Lawrence University, Appleton, Wisconsin.

Thessaly. The latter had fled, accompanied by a handful of loyal men. Since Egypt was only a few days away by ship, and since young King Ptolemy owed him considerable favors, he decided to sail there with a small fleet in the hope of finding a logistical base for his revenge on Caesar.

On July 25, he arrived in sight of Ptolemy's camp, which was not at Pelusium itself but at Mount Kasios, a high, sandy mound some fifty miles east of the city. Pompey's unexpected arrival plunged the royal council into a quandary. The courtiers who composed it occupy a special place in the accounts of these events. For us, the court of the Lagide monarchs remains for the most part a murky affair, but this instance is an exception that finds its explanation in the major—and sinister—role these personages played. First and foremost, there was Pothinos, a eunuch according to our sources. He was both head of the regency council and in charge of the administration of finances. Along with him were the commandant of the army, Achillas, and the young king's tutor Theodotos of Chios. Judging Pompey's cause to be hopeless, the three decided to side with the victor and, to attract the latter's good graces, to murder the fugitive.

Plutarch's detailed account is especially poignant.[23] Achillas assumed responsibility for the sordid affair: Accompanied by two officers from Gabinius's former army, he set out for Pompey's galley in a humble fishing boat. Dark premonitions notwithstanding, the general agreed to go on board. The moment they set foot on the shore, he was run through from behind by the military tribune Septimius under the horrified gaze of his followers and his wife, Cornelia, who, powerless, observed the scene from their vessel. The despicable nature of this crime weighed, in a certain way unfairly, on the memory of the young Ptolemy to the extent that Dante reserved a place of honor for him in his Inferno. In the context of the moment, this act, odious though it was, was far from unjustified. As Plutarch has the king's tutor say, to accept Pompey or to reject him were two equally dangerous options that risked shifting the Roman civil war onto Egyptian soil. The conspirators' biggest mistakes were undoubtedly the awkwardness with which the murder was carried out, before so many witnesses who could report the contemptible circumstances, and the crude manner in which they then attempted to exploit their deed before Caesar.

The latter disembarked at Alexandria two days later, on July 27. He was accompanied by two legions that had been reduced to 3,200 men and by 800 cavalry. Left to itself since the king and his council departed for combat, the city was in turmoil, and tension mounted with the arrival of the Romans. Caesar shut himself up in the royal palace, where he soon learned of the death of his enemy. For their part, Pothinos and Theodotos, informed of the illustrious visitor, hurried to the capital, leaving the army at Pelusium under the charge of Achillas and bringing with them the head and the seal of their victim.[24] The tears of Caesar when he beheld the macabre trophy were scarcely convincing. He was undoubtedly thrilled to be finally rid of this major obstacle blocking his route to absolute power without having to bear responsibility for the assassination of the greatest leader of his day, but he could not reward the treachery to which this illustrious citizen of Rome had fallen victim. Thus, far from attracting gratitude, Ptolemy's party earned only mistrust and loathing.

Though the initial purpose of his arrival in Egypt was now out of the way, and despite the threat that a Pompeian party deprived of its leader but still powerful could pose to the outcome of the civil war, Caesar opted to remain at Alexandria. The historians of antiquity judged this decision rather harshly: The great strategist had shut himself up in a trap, taking considerable risk for no better reason than the alluring eyes of Cleopatra. Caesar defended himself from such an accusation by claiming that he "was unable to move because of the prevailing northwest winds which at this time make it impossible to get out of Alexandria."[25] In proffering such an excuse, Caesar wished especially to minimize the financial and political aspects of his stay, which could have shocked the Roman public. His immediate motive was in fact sordid enough. Since the beginning of his ambitious career, Caesar had been in constant search of financial sources, cash being the indispensable means of assuring both the loyalty of his legions and the assistance of his allies and political supporters. Moreover, he had accepted responsibility for the debts owed to the banker Rabirius Postumus for the sums borrowed by Ptolemy XII during his exile in Rome. The time had come for the king of Egypt to pay his predecessor's debts. Further, Caesar sought material assistance similar to that which the Egyptian sovereigns had accorded to the son of Pompey the previous year. Since he had to contend with the predictable ill will of the king's ministers, as well as with the hostility of an Alexandrian population fearful of being burdened with new costs linked to the reimbursement of the debt and the payment of a heavy tribute, he realized that he could not achieve his goals except by settling the unstable political situation. Egypt's riches were in fact so great, as was the potential power of the person who could control them, that he needed to make himself master of the land.

He therefore resolved to impose his arbitration, convoking the two conflicting parties at Alexandria. Pothinos, however, justly afraid of paying the cost of a possible reconciliation, was conducting psychological warfare, delivering rotten grain to the Roman soldiers under the pretext that the granaries were empty, and using all sorts of means to stir up antipathy toward Rome in Alexandria and its environs. When the king and his court finally arrived at the palace, they were served from pottery vessels, Pothinos insinuating that Caesar had seized all the precious metal plate.

Meanwhile, Cleopatra was blocked from traveling to the capital by the army of Achillas, which held Pelusium, and by the strict measures that Pothinos had taken to monitor access to Alexandria by land and by sea. Nevertheless, she had managed to get a message through to the Roman, and the response she had received seemed encouraging; still, she could hope for nothing so long as her enemies had free run of the palace. Informed of Caesar's notorious taste for pretty women, she attempted a brilliant but audacious stroke that has been famous ever since, from Plutarch's account down through modern film productions. Slipping through Achillas's blockade at night, she followed the coastline by ship as far as the suburbs of the capital. There, she hid in a humble boat under the conduct of a man she could trust, a Sicilian named Apollodoros. Somehow, the latter succeeded in eluding the vigilance of the sentinels and in bringing the queen, wrapped in a carpet, into the private quarters of the dictator.

Reports of the clever staging of this appearance are likely authentic, considering the artifices that Cleopatra later employed to charm both individuals and crowds. On this occasion, Cleopatra adroitly mixed seduction and compassion, combining personal display with a disarray of clothing that suited the circumstances. Caesar's reaction was precisely the opposite of that provoked by the king's courtiers when they presented him with the head of his former colleague. Cleopatra's seductive and intelligent conversation conquered the man who had vanquished both the Gauls and Pompey. Nevertheless, this man in his fifties, who had survived all sorts of experiences, could not allow intoxication of the senses to gain the upper hand over good political sense: He decided to adhere strictly to the provisions of Auletes' testament, with no special favoritism toward Cleopatra. In all likelihood, moreover, she had the wits not to ask for more.

With his customary promptitude, when dawn broke, Caesar summoned the young Ptolemy to a definitive arbitration. When he saw his hated sister parading alongside the Roman, the adolescent threw a fit. He left the palace crying treason, and, in front of a crowd that his shouts had attracted, he hurled his royal headband to the ground. Though the raving boy was quickly seized and led back into the palace enclosure, the emotion of a crowd already white-hot thanks to Pothinos's propaganda turned to riot. Only Caesar's eloquence calmed the frenzy, at the cost of some vague promises that temporarily assuaged the aroused spirits. Before the assembled people and in the presence of the two rivals, he read Ptolemy XII's testament, stressing the role the latter had assigned to the Romans in regard to its execution.

Not only did he impose a reconciliation between Ptolemy and Cleopatra, but, by his own authority, he restored Cyprus to the Lagide dynasty, installing the youngest of the deceased king's children, Ptolemy XIV and Arsinoe, as sovereigns of the island. By returning this territory, annexed a dozen years earlier, Caesar was attempting to heal the blow to their self-esteem that this seizure had caused the people of Alexandria, hoping thus to end the hatred the latter had felt for the Romans ever since. This decision proved to be one of the many miscalculations he made during his stay in Egypt, for his concession was interpreted as a sign of weakness.

The Alexandrian War

For some weeks, the dynastic crisis seemed to be settled, as attested by a Demotic inscription written in a temple at Thebes on September 17, 48, and dated to "pharaoh Ptolemy (XIII) and pharaoh Cleopatra (VII), the gods who love their father."[26] The Egyptian priests who wrote this text evidently could not have been informed of the latest events that had occurred more than six hundred miles away at the capital. The royal army under Achillas's command had begun to march toward Alexandria, undoubtedly at the instigation of the minister Pothinos, who, seeing his position ever more threatened by Caesar's initiatives, hoped to catch the latter unprepared and to drive him into the sea.

Thus broke out the famous Alexandrian war, of which Caesar himself left a detailed account that was completed by one of his lieutenants. As for Cleopatra, she played almost no part in this affair that pitted Caesar's meager troops against Achillas's Greco-Egyptian army for four months. It was a heated struggle between the Roman, who was entrenched with the royal family in the palace quarter, and an enemy far greater in number who enjoyed the active support of the population. Caesar's most audacious attempt to escape this tight spot was setting fire to the Egyptian fleet in the Great Port, a fire that spread to the neighboring quays and buildings. Did all the intellectual treasures of the great Library go up in smoke on this occasion, or only a warehouse filled with books destined for export? The question remains open, though the second thesis is the one that is now favored.

Whatever the case, this exploit did not end the fighting. The quarrels of the Lagide family and the dissension among the leaders of the insurrection proved to be trump cards for the dictator, however. Arsinoe, Cleopatra's younger sister, managed to escape from the palace and to join the camp of its besiegers, where she was recognized as queen, while her tutor, the eunuch Ganymede, contended with Achillas over the leadership of the operations. After the execution of Pothinos, whose maneuvers in support of his accomplice Achillas had been discovered, and the assassination of the latter by Ganymede, Caesar decided to expel Ptolemy in the hope of increasing confusion in the enemy camp. The long-awaited reinforcements led by Mithridates of Pergamon finally arrived, along with Jewish contingents led by Antipater, minister of the high priest of Jerusalem and father of the future king Herod. The decisive battle took place outside Alexandria, on the Canopic branch of the Nile, where the Egyptians, who were trying to intercept the relief army, were surprised by a maneuver of Caesar, who attacked them from the rear. The death of the young king, who drowned while attempting to cross the river in an overloaded boat, led to the surrender of the Egyptian army on January 15, 47. Caesar ordered a search for the body to belie any rumor of the king's survival. The only thing recovered, however, was the gilded cuirass that Ptolemy had worn during the battle; it was put on display as a trophy in the sight of the people of Alexandria.

As was his custom, Caesar showed himself magnanimous, pardoning without a second thought enemies now without a leader and thus rendered harmless. By his right as conqueror, he could have proclaimed the annexation of Egypt, but such a measure would evidently have entailed more risks than advantages. In particular, annexation would have required entrusting the new province—the richest and most populous in the empire—to someone both qualified and steadfastly loyal, two qualities that were at that time practically a contradiction. He therefore announced his intention of respecting, as he had done until then, the provisions of the testament of Ptolemy XII. The latter's older son having perished, he was replaced by his younger brother, Ptolemy XIV, who with Cleopatra formed the new royal couple. This association was purely formal, for everyone knew that Cleopatra, fortified by Caesar's favor, would alone hold the effective power, a fact that the royal protocol demonstrated from that time on by placing the queen's name first.

Whatever else he might have wished to do, Caesar could scarcely remain any longer in Egypt. New challenges must have been quickly noted: In addition to the menace posed by the rallying of the Pompeians in Africa, Asia Minor was witnessing the aggressive exploits of Pharnakes, king of the Cimmerian Bosporos, who was reviving the sinister glory of his father, Mithridates, the most implacable enemy Rome had known. Did

Caesar, despite all, take time for a pleasure cruise on the Nile, accompanied by the queen and escorted by his legions, as claimed nearly two centuries later by Appian[27] and Suetonius?[28] The latter insists that the dictator intended to go all the way to Ethiopia, but the circumstances—the army refused to accompany him that far—are an obvious reminiscence of the saga of Alexander, whose soldiers prevented him from pursuing the conquest of India. The suspicion aroused by the anecdote is reinforced by the apparent denial reported by the Caesarian writer of *Alexandrian War*,[29] though the chronological uncertainties regarding Caesar's departure for Syria do not enable us to decide. If good sense stands in the way of our imagining a lengthy voyage that would scarcely have been opportune in the context of the moment, a triumphal excursion to Memphis, the ancient capital of the pharaohs, would seem plausible. The mere presence in that city of the new sovereigns and their eminent protector would have guaranteed them the allegiance of the entire population of Egypt, thanks to the mediation of the clergy of Ptah, who alone were authorized to administer the traditional rites of a pharaonic coronation. In this way Caesar could have achieved the pacification of Egypt that he had undertaken.

For added security, Caesar left behind no fewer than three legions, thus demonstrating the place he intended to reserve for Egypt in his new organization of the Roman world, that of a closely controlled protectorate. The command of this army was left to Rufio, a humble knight whose modest origins—his father had been a mere freedman—conveniently limited the ambitions that military control over such a rich country might have awakened in someone of higher birth.

The New Aphrodite

Cleopatra in Rome

In his propaganda, Caesar highlighted the amazing panache with which he defeated Pharnakes at Zela (*veni, vidi, vici*) and then the Pompeians at Thapsos. When he was able to return to Rome in May 46, rid of nearly all his enemies, he summoned the Egyptian sovereigns. From the latters' point of view, such a journey was scarcely called for. Eastern kings and princes normally came to Rome only as suppliants or hostages. Cleopatra and her young husband were obviously not those sorts of visitors, though they might have hoped their trip would result in official recognition by the senate as "friends and allies of the Roman People." Only Caesar could hope to find advantage in a presence that demonstrated before the eyes of all his personal hold over Egypt and its dynasty—and also enabled him to maintain his ties with the bewitching queen of Egypt.

Cleopatra might have arrived in time to be present at the four triumphs[1] that the dictator celebrated successively in this year of 46. If that was the case, we can only imagine her mixed emotions before the spectacle of her sister Arsinoe covered with chains and exposed thus to the curiosity of the commoners of Rome. The sympathetic outburst of the crowd, aroused by the courage and the dignity of the young prisoner, could have vexed the queen, all the more so as Caesar, with care for his own image, quickly responded to this unexpected reaction by freeing the princess, who found refuge in the temple of Artemis at Ephesos. Unfortunately, we have almost no specifics regarding Cleopatra's stay in Rome, except that Caesar scarcely tried to disguise the nature of his relationship with the Egyptian queen, going so far as to lodge the royal couple on his own estate, a vast domain on the right bank of the Tiber, in the well-to-do part of the city. Aside from some echoes of scandal provoked by a doubly adulterous liaison,[2] and two or three bitter remarks by Cicero, who was entirely opposed to the queen,[3] the rest is left to our imagination.

Ever since antiquity, Cleopatra's hold on the master of Rome has been a matter of debate. Some rumors told of impossible plans to transfer the seat of power to Alexandria. Others bruited that Caesar had prepared an official decree permitting him to be polygamous,[4] and thus to marry Cleopatra, but no such text was ever made public. In fact, all this malicious gossip finds corroboration in only a single, enigmatic act: Caesar placed a gilded statue of Cleopatra in the sanctuary of Venus the Mother—*Genetrix,* the divine ancestor of his own line—at the center of the new forum that he had presented to the Roman people at his own expense.[5] Dedicating a statue in a temple to a sovereign or to a distinguished individual was a widespread practice in the Hellenistic East, where this form of homage was held in high esteem. We may imagine that in Rome, rendering such an honor to a foreign queen was not to the taste of all, but it is clear that this was but one small object of discontent in the context of many innovations undermining republican tradition and making the Roman state seem more and more like an Eastern monarchy.

Many historians have wished to see the influence of the queen of Egypt in the great reforms that Caesar undertook during the two years when he held sole power. It is true that some of them were inspired by Hellenistic, even purely Egyptian, models. An example is the reform of the calendar. Like most ancient peoples, the Romans calculated time in lunar years of 355 days, which obliged them to add a month to certain years in order to prevent the seasons from shifting. These intercalations were left to the pontiffs, who often neglected to make them, however, resulting in major discrepancies. Caesar drew his inspiration from the traditional solar calendar of the Egyptians, whose year had 365 days; the synod convened by King Ptolemy III at Canopus in 238 had decided to improve this calendar by adding one extra day every four years but did not succeed in putting this reform into practice in Egypt. On the advice of the Alexandrian astronomer and mathematician Sosigenes,[6] Caesar adopted this system as his own, imposing on Rome the so-called "Julian" year. This system is the basis of our own calendar, with some minor adjustments due to Pope Gregory XIII in the sixteenth century of our own era. Although some scholars see an imitation of the Alexandrian model in the project of creating public libraries that was placed in the hands of Varro,[7] many such institutions already existed throughout the Hellenistic world. Likewise, the plan to drain the Pomptine marshes or to divert the Tiber by means of a canal doubtless owed nothing to Egyptian hydrologic projects, though these have also been claimed; the natural conditions of the two lands are too different for such a parallel to be valid.

A critical review of the sources does not permit us to affirm that Caesar was in large part inspired by his Egyptian mistress in his political projects, much less that he was reserving an important place for her in the future constitution of the empire. Quite the contrary, it is possible to write a biography of Caesar in which his liaison with Cleopatra was nothing more than a brief affair.[8] In any event, we must beware of retrojecting the designs we can attribute to Mark Antony and the queen a dozen years later, just before Actium. As for Caesar, he had neither the time nor, undoubtedly, the intent to write a political testament, a circumstance that prevents us from ever knowing his true plans.

Return to the Land of the Nile

Caesar's last months belong exclusively to the history of Rome. Cleopatra was but a powerless spectator before the succession of events that ended in the ultimate tragedy of the Ides of March, 44. This event ended whatever hopes she might have entertained in her liaison with the dictator. The disclosure of his testament could scarcely have met her expectations, though none of its dispositions concerned her expressly. Cleopatra could not have been unaware that Roman law forbade any citizen from making a bequest to a foreigner. The principal heir was the young Octavian, one of Caesar's great-nephews, who thus also became his adoptive son. According to Suetonius, though, in this same testament, Caesar designated guardians for "the son who might be born to him."[9] By what woman could the dictator have expected a child when he wrote his last wishes on September 13, 45? Certainly not Calpurnia, his legitimate wife, who had remained barren throughout their fourteen years of marriage. It is likely that this clause was written with Cleopatra in mind, though she was not mentioned by name.

Though the situation in Rome had become uncertain and dangerous, Cleopatra waited several weeks before leaving the city. In fact, it was not until April 15 that Cicero wrote to his friend Atticus, "The queen's flight does not pain me."[10] To the time she needed for preparations must doubtless be added some diplomatic maneuvers that were necessary at such a critical juncture. Cleopatra was near term, which might have made her hesitate to undertake such a journey too quickly. She must have decided to leave to avoid becoming the hostage of one or the other of the parties that were rushing inevitably toward a new civil war. On the journey, doubtless during a stopover in Greece, she gave birth to a son, who was immediately named Caesar.[11] This extraordinary news was dispatched as quickly as possible to Rome, where it arrived by May 11[12] but found little reaction. There was already an adoptive son of Caesar, named as heir by the deceased's own testament, and a single Caesar was quite enough, both for the friends of the young Octavian, who had himself just arrived in Rome, and for the partisans of the dictator's assassins. In any case, Roman law stipulated that a child born to a foreign woman could not be legitimate, while the clause in Caesar's will concerning a future son was insufficiently clear to be considered a recognition. The idea of a recognition was, however, argued before the senate by Mark Antony in the hope that this stratagem might block the spirited ambitions that his young adversary based solely on his posthumous adoption. Though he could cite witnesses, Antony did not succeed in convincing, and he gave up his efforts.[13]

For their part, Cleopatra and her retinue did not land at Alexandria before July. First, the queen had to stop over on Cyprus, an episode that the historians of antiquity, evidently absorbed by the initiatives of the various protagonists in the impending civil war, did not deem worth recounting. Although Cyprus had been, at least in theory, restored to the Lagide dynasty by Caesar at the time of the Alexandrian war, the exact status of the territory remained uncertain.[14] The troubled situation in the spring of 44 finally offered Cleopatra an excellent opportunity to restore her authority over an island whose destiny had so long been linked to that of her ancestors. Moreover, she had to counter the intrigues hatched by her hated sister Arsinoe, who was attempting to gain control over a possession that Caesar himself had awarded to her in October 48. The operation, whose details are not all known to us, was an out-and-out success. The return of Cyprus to the Egyptian bosom was commemorated by an issue of bronze coins that opportunely depicted the queen holding her newborn son in her arms.[15] To govern the island, she left behind one of the loyal partisans who made up her little court during her stay at Rome, a certain Serapion whose arrogance had been little appreciated by Cicero at that time.[16]

As soon as she arrived in Alexandria, Cleopatra rid herself of the brother whom Caesar had imposed on her as coregent three years earlier. The sources are clear on this point, in particular the testimony of Flavius Josephus:[17] It is scarcely possible to clear Cleopatra of this heinous crime. The adolescent was at that time about fifteen years of age, and Cleopatra doubtless feared a return of the situation in 49–48, when she had been compelled to abandon the throne to her other brother, Ptolemy XIII. Moreover, the birth of Caesarion had overturned the facts of Egyptian politics. She immediately advertised the paternity of the infant, rendering her union with her brother de facto null and void. The latter then became a bothersome rival who not only had good reason to contest the child's right to succeed him, but who was also in a position to turn to Arsinoe, whom Caesar had spared, to replace his adulterous wife. To head off this double danger, Cleopatra had recourse to this purely precautionary crime, following what had become a classic scenario in the Hellenistic royal families and among the Lagides in particular, but which could still shock republican Romans, accustomed though they were to so many other horrors.

With Ptolemy XIV eliminated, Cleopatra was sole sovereign for a time. Having a son at hand, though he was only a few months old, she did not have to search for a husband, as other queens in the same situation had been obliged to do.[18] She had only to await the propitious moment to have this child recognized as king, though she herself would remain the dominant figure in the new royal partnership.

For the moment, though, the country was not in a favorable situation. In addition to the three legions left behind by Caesar to maintain order, there was a fourth whose origin remains unknown.[19] We can easily imagine the burden these soldiers placed on the economic resources of the country, along with the problems of their coexistence with the local population, whether Egyptian or Hellenized. By chance, this inopportune occupation ended less than a year after the return of the royal court to Alexandria.

The high officials the queen had left behind during her absence proved to be loyal and competent, at least enough so that she did not deem it necessary to replace them. Such was the case with the Alexandrian Theon,[20] who was in charge of the central administration, and especially with Callimachos, the *epistrategos* of the Thebais—that is, the governor of Upper Egypt.[21] But more than human malice, it was the hostility of nature that would torment Egypt in these difficult times. Starting in 43, the population was afflicted by famine and pestilence. The years 42 and 41 were especially bad: The Nile inundation, the sole guarantor of agricultural production in Egypt, was entirely absent for two years in a row, an exceptional phenomenon that could have seemed like a veritable curse sent down by the gods. At other times, such a circumstance would have been enough to provoke major social disorder, or even a general revolt. Yet this did not happen, thanks in part to the zealousness of some of the officials. Measures taken by Callimachos were commemorated on a stela set up in his honor by the priests of Amun at Thebes.[22]

Other officials reacted to the general stagnation in a more classic and inappropriate manner, by attempting to make up the inevitable loss to the royal treasury by means of various exactions. When these exactions hit the weakest and the most impoverished, these had no recourse other than flight, but when the victims were the temples or well-to-do landowners, complaints reached the highest levels. Cleopatra herself felt obliged to intervene between her officials and certain of her privileged subjects. In particular, many citizens of Alexandria had fields in the countryside that were normally exempted from the exceptional taxes that were levied in times of crisis. A royal decree dated to 41 provided that henceforth, employees of the tax bureau were forbidden to ignore these time-honored exemptions.[23] In defending such immunities, the crown intended to conciliate the wealthy bourgeoisie of Alexandria, whose backing it needed, both for its own security in the capital and for its conduct of foreign policy. From that time on, the latter would monopolize the attention of the queen and her counselors, for Egypt was about to be drawn into the agony of the Roman civil war.

Cleopatra and Caesar's Murderers

The confusion that marked the events of 44–43 in the West was essentially the result of dissension among the various pretenders to Caesar's heritage, a situation that enabled the republicans to organize and to strengthen themselves. The two leaders of the conspiracy against Caesar established themselves in the East: Brutus in Macedonia and Cassius in Syria. The latter province was also coveted by Dolabella, one of the Caesarian leaders. Short of troops, he sent his deputy Allienus to secure the four legions that had been occupying Egypt since 47.[24] Cleopatra caused no difficulty with regard to their departure, but on his return from Egypt, Allienus was intercepted by Cassius, who was thus able to add these four legions to his own already considerable army. Since Dolabella, despite all, gained the advantage in a first naval engagement, Cassius was obliged to request vessels from all the maritime provinces of the East, from Rhodes to Egypt. Knowing that the balance of forces favored the republican, several of those who were asked complied; some, such as the Rhodians and the Lycians, invoked their neutrality; and Cleopatra evinced a more ambiguous attitude. She offered the excuse that the condition of her land, which was ravaged by famine and pestilence, did not permit her to send the fleet that had been requested; later, she claimed that she had been preparing to aid Dolabella, but that contrary winds had prevented her from doing so.[25]

Allegedly without the queen's knowledge, Serapion, the Egyptian governor of Cyprus, dispatched ships to Cassius. This action does not necessarily imply treason on Serapion's part, but rather that Cleopatra was playing a double game that has taken in so many ancient and modern historians. Though her past actions distanced her from the faction of Caesar's assassins, Cleopatra was deciding her course of action only in terms of the interests of her kingdom. Since circumstances seemed to favor the republicans, she could not risk declaring herself to be their enemy, but her strategy became a matter of not aiding them directly. Serapion became the victim of this dangerous game. In aiding Cassius, he left Cleopatra complete latitude to approve of his action or to disavow it, depending on the outcome of the conflict.

Thanks to the reinforcements he obtained, Cassius was finally able to triumph over Dolabella, who committed suicide in July 43. Master of the East, the victor turned his attention toward Egypt, whose riches, real or supposed, were ever coveted by Roman generals short of resources. Curiously, it was the very alibi furnished by Cleopatra—the distress inflicted on her land by natural disasters—that inspired him to view Egypt as easy prey.[26] By chance, as Cassius was preparing an invasion, Brutus summoned him to Smyrna for an emergency conference. Antony and Octavian had finally reconciled, forming, along with Lepidus, a new triumvirate on November 11, 43, and they were preparing to lead their troops into Greece to confront the republicans. At that time, the triumvirs issued a decree recognizing little Caesarion's royal title, under the pretext of rewarding his mother for the assistance, real or intended, she had given to the unfortunate Dolabella.[27] The object of this concession was evidently to obtain, cheaply, the alliance of Egypt. Cleopatra, understanding that she could not disappoint their expectations, hastily mounted an expedition to join the Caesarian faction in the Adriatic. Cassius attempted to prevent the forces from linking by sending a fleet to Cape Tainaron at the southern tip of the Peloponnesos to intercept Cleopatra's vessels. This was a needless precaution, for a storm routed the Egyptian armada off the Libyan coast, forcing the queen, who was seasick, to return to Alexandria in a sorry state.[28] Cleopatra had no opportunity to make a fresh attempt, for Antony and Octavian successively crushed the armies of Cassius and Brutus in the two battles of Philippi in Macedonia in October 42. The republicans were definitively beaten.

The victory of the Caesarian party, to which her past linked her, must have pleased the queen, though she also found in it reasons for worry. She had barely aided her benefactor's avengers, and her conduct could justly be viewed as equivocal. Moreover, she knew that the recognition granted to her son had been dictated by purely tactical considerations, and that it in no way implied a favorable attitude on the part of the triumvirs under these new circumstances.

Mark Antony

When the provinces of the empire were divided after the defeat of the republicans, Mark Antony received responsibility for the East, with charge over the states and the allied kingdoms, foremost of which was Egypt. Then at the age of about forty, he enjoyed great popularity both at Rome and in the provinces. Before joining Caesar, he had served as a cavalry prefect under the proconsul of Syria, Aulus Gabinius, and in this position he had played an important role in the expedition that restored Ptolemy XII, Cleopatra's father, to the throne of Egypt.[29] This occasion revealed his spirited courage and his tactical genius, but it was his generous and chivalrous attitude that brought him the most renown. He had opposed the reprisals that the sovereign wished to heap on his subjects, while at the same time seeing to the royal funeral of Ptolemy's enemy Archelaos, the husband of the unfortunate queen Berenike IV. The effusive gratitude that Antony received from the Alexandrians at that time contrasted with the passionate hatred they displayed toward Caesar some years later. Antony was able to compensate for his evident political and strategic deficiencies with an incontestable humanity that always won the hearts of others and which seems to have been singularly lacking in his mentor, Caesar. Nevertheless, he became the most loyal of the latter's companions, from the time of the Gallic war on, to the point of being named Master of the Horse when Caesar assumed his first dictatorship in 48.

Subsequently, relations between the two men became strained because of the dissipated and scandalous life that Antony was leading in the idleness of Rome. And yet it was Antony who, during the festival of the Lupercalia on February 15, 44, led an attempted coup d'état to confer the royal office on Caesar.[30] We know how the dictator, hesitating on this occasion to cross such a Rubicon, refused the crown that his young colleague tendered to him. Placed in the second rank of Caesar's heirs, Antony had to confront both the republicans and the partisans of Octavian, until the accord he negotiated with the latter finally enabled him to avenge Caesar's ghost by driving the instigators of his assassination to their deaths.

Antony spent the winter of 42–41 in Greece, where he increased his popularity by advertising a sincere interest in Hellenism, though he used this interest to cover many exactions intended to finance the bonuses he had promised his soldiers. He then moved on to rich Asia Minor, where not only did his exactions increase at the expense of the local communities, but also his pretensions to divinity, which were encouraged by the enthusiasm of the crowds and the obligingness of his flatterers. He was a new Dionysos, a new Herakles, whose distant descendent he boasted he was. Sumptuous displays were staged to convince the local populations, such as the procession that marked his entry into Ephesus; the procession was headed by bacchants and satyrs dancing to the music of flutes and panpipes in streets decorated with *thyrsi* and ivy.[31]

But this assimilation to Dionysos had far more reason than to justify the lifestyle that Antony would lead from that time on. It was first and foremost a matter of conditioning minds for the war he was planning against the Parthians and of placing himself at the forefront of this grandiose project. In fact, a dozen years earlier, Parthians had crushed the Roman army and killed the triumvir Crassus. In the meanwhile, they had posed a constant danger to the interests of Rome in eastern Asia Minor and in Syria-Palestine, in particular dominating the Armenian kingdom that Pompey had once reduced to a protectorate. Furthermore, the Parthians had always supported the anti-Caesarians during the civil wars. Caesar was preparing an expedition against them at the time of his death,[32] and its success would have permitted him to become a new Alexander; Antony felt he could accomplish this much, now that the civil war was over and his enemies routed. But realizing this dream would require more than just identifying himself with Dionysos departing for his conquest of India; rather, it would be necessary to mobilize all the forces of the East. The cooperation of Egypt was therefore indispensable to him.

The Encounter at Tarsos

Settled at Tarsos in Cilicia, one of the few eastern cities that had resisted Cassius' exactions, Antony summoned Cleopatra through the mediation of his personal envoy, Quintus Dellius.[33] The queen was to come and explain her attitude during the recent conflict and perhaps suffer the consequences. Had she previously met Antony? This is what most of her modern biographers suppose—some going so far as to imagine a previous liaison—but with no confirmation from the ancient sources. Their paths could have crossed at Alexandria in 55, when Antony, under Gabinius's orders, led Ptolemy XII back into his palace. But Cleopatra was still a girl of fourteen and the love at first sight mentioned by Appian in connection with this early meeting seems to be nothing more than a fiction invented after the fact.[34] As for their possible relations in Rome between 46 and 44, while the queen was holding her salon in Caesar's villa, they must have been so distant that they were in no way the talk of the town. Quite the contrary, Plutarch's account presents a Dellius informing Cleopatra of Antony's character and dispositions, which implies that she hardly knew him. Yet the manipulative role that Plutarch imputes to Dellius on this occasion seems highly exaggerated. Cleopatra was surely the sole originator of the sumptuous production that would transport her destiny to the level of myth.

While Cleopatra's entry into history as a girl emerging from a carpet before a stupefied Caesar was a minor masterpiece of feigned improvisation and calculated modesty, her appearance before Antony at Tarsos (Figure 3) was, by contrast, an impressive spectacle that was carefully and lavishly prepared. Meanwhile, Plutarch informs us, she had passed from the inexperience of youth to a "time of life when women's beauty is most splendid

Figure 3. Gérard de Lairesse, *The Landing of Cleopatra at Tarsos.* The Louvre. Photo by H. Lewandowski, courtesy of Réunion des Musées Nationaux/Art Resource, New York.

and their intellects are in full maturity."[35] In fact, both the circumstances and the personalities of the Roman leaders she set out to seduce were quite different in the two cases, and she succeeded in finding just the right method with each of them.

The fleet that journeyed up the river Kydnos to Tarsos was prodigious and arrogant. Gliding along on the calm waters and surrounded by exquisite aromas, Cleopatra reclined under a gold-embroidered dais atop the gilded stern of a vessel with purple sails. Boys dressed as Cupids stood on each side of her, while her crew, who plied oars of silver, was composed exclusively of women dressed as Nereids and Graces. It was indeed the epiphany of a goddess that was beheld by the people who dwelled along the river and by the inhabitants of the city. The latter all rushed toward the quay where these supernatural visitors were about to dock, leaving Antony alone on the tribunal where he was holding audience. This luxurious arrival was the introduction to one of those sumptuous banquets that would forever after be linked with the name of Cleopatra. The queen had in fact seen to everything, down to the thousands of lights ingeniously arranged so as to transform the ship into a sparkling jewel in the night, illuminating the guests.[36]

Far from offending the triumvir, this display flattered his pride. Presenting herself before him as a goddess rather than a suppliant vassal, Cleopatra reinforced Antony's conviction of his own divine essence, which had been revealed to him by his enthusiastic reception in Asia. This was no longer an ordinary diplomatic matter, but rather the mystic encounter of Aphrodite and Dionysos, with the well-being of the East at stake. At a time when the tumult of arms seemed never ending, and when the expectation of a savior had spread everywhere as the sole hope for populations fallen prey to the worst of afflictions, the brilliance of an event so rich in symbols seemed to herald a new Golden Age.

We can easily imagine that the misunderstandings with regard to Cleopatra's attitude during the recent civil war were quickly cleared up. Antony undoubtedly imposed some restrictions on Cleopatra's rule over Cyprus, whose governor, Serapion, had conveniently fled to Phoenicia, making it possible for his former sovereign to grant Antony the responsibility for his extradition and punishment. For the rest, Cleopatra requested and obtained the elimination of her sister Arsinoe, who was still in asylum in the temple of Ephesos, as well as the execution of a false Ptolemy XIII who had thrown the citizens of Arados into turmoil.[37] With her position thus reinforced, she returned to her kingdom with Antony's promise to join her in Alexandria as soon as he finished settling affairs in the East. The most important of these matters, the projected expedition against the Parthians, was postponed until the coming year, despite the threat of an attack by the latter, who had been roused to action by the republican general Labienus, who betrayed his country and took refuge with King Orodes II.

The Pleasures of the "Inimitable Life"

Antony thus seemed to be sacrificing the interests of Rome at Cleopatra's invitation when he hastened to Alexandria, where he spent the winter of 41–40. While Caesar's stay in the capital of Egypt seven years earlier aroused some reservations, that of his successor is unanimously condemned by our sources. The triumvir is regarded as having succumbed to the realm of the senses to the point of neglecting his mission and his duties, leaving the East insufficiently organized and paying no attention to the serious events being hatched in the West. Even taking account of the partial and retrospective judgment passed on this episode by Octavian's propaganda in the years 33–31, which we find repeated by later historians, it is difficult to comprehend the political motives behind Antony's conduct, if indeed there were any. Granted, the season was scarcely conducive to military operations, and while Alexandria was not the strategically best place to take up winter quarters, it would at least prove to be the most pleasant.

Cleopatra's display of luxury at Tarsos had been but a foretaste of what awaited Antony at Alexandria (Figure 4). The queen omitted no artifice to astound the Roman, putting all the riches and resources of her land at his disposal. Now ranked among the

Figure 4. Jan De Bray, *Banquet of Antony and Cleopatra,* 1669. Currier Funds 1969.8.
Photo by Bill Finney, courtesy of The Currier Gallery of Art, Manchester, New
Hampshire.

gods, Antony could no longer lead the life of a simple mortal. This new lifestyle, which would display to the world the *tryphe* (magnificence) of the new master and mistress of the East, was incarnated in the famous circle of the "Inimitable Life,"[38] an association that included the two lovers and some close associates deemed worthy of this honor. These associates included a certain Aphrodisios who, qualifying himself as a "parasite" of Antony, dedicated a statue to the latter, "Great and Inimitable, his god and benefactor."[39] We can see that such pretensions were well-intentioned and mitigated by humor, an eminent quality that Plutarch readily ascribes to Antony. This self-deprecating humor made it possible for the "Inimitables" to go slumming, disguised as servants, in the dives of Alexandria, at the risk of being roughed up in some nocturnal brawl. But despite what was claimed by the later propaganda, Cleopatra's intention was not to exploit the influence she had obtained over Antony to weaken him and to render him harmless. Quite the contrary, she missed no opportunity to arouse his ambition and his will to conquer, as is well illustrated by the quip that, according to Plutarch, she tossed at him on the occasion of a fishing trip: "Leave the fishing-rod, general, to us poor sovereigns of Pharos and Canopus; your game is cities, provinces, and kingdoms."[40]

Such exhortations were not unneeded, for the situation at the beginning of the year 40 seemed extremely dangerous. The Parthian armies, led by Pakoros, the heir to the throne, and by the Roman felon Labienus, were advancing rapidly in Syria and Asia Minor, all the more so because Antony had left no troops to defend these provinces other than those of the defeated republican party. As Labienus had in fact been one of the leaders of the party, the troops thus had no scruples about going over to the enemy. Apamea fell, and then Antioch. In the north, after occupying Cilicia, Labienus pressed forward as far as Caria, reaching the shores of the Aegean, while in the south, Pakoros had expelled the Jewish high priest Hyrkanos II, whom Antony had just confirmed in power, and replaced him with his own creature, Antigonos. All the East seemed to be falling into the hands of the Parthians.

Cleopatra in the Shadows

Without waiting for winter to end, Antony embarked for Tyre, one of the few Phoenician ports still putting up a resistance. There, he received still more alarming news, this time from Italy. At the instigation of his wife, Fulvia, his brother Lucius Antonius had entered into armed conflict with Octavian. The origin of the problem was Octavian's sudden decision to reintegrate, to his own sole advantage, the veterans of the recent wars. To this end, he had appropriated properties both large and small to settle more than a hundred thousand of his own demobilized soldiers on the confiscated lands, without giving any thought to Antony's veterans, who were also quite numerous in the West. Fulvia, a woman who was devoured by a thoroughly virile ambition, had judged it opportune to take advantage of the anger of the dispossessed property owners and of the ex-soldiers who had been left without a share to render a service to Antony by getting rid of Octavian.

This new civil war, initiated without Antony's knowledge, had quickly turned into a rout for the latter's relatives. Besieged in Perugia, Lucius was obliged to capitulate, while Fulvia fled to Greece. Caught between two fires, Antony deemed it more urgent to occupy himself first with affairs in the West. From Tyre, he set sail for Athens, where he met Fulvia and heaped reproaches on her for her temerity. Then, after drawing together enough troops and ships, he disembarked in Italy, ready to fight it out with Octavian. The latter preferred to compromise and engaged in lengthy negotiations that ended in an accord concluded at Brindisium in October 40. The triumvirate was reconstituted on its former bases. Moreover, since Fulvia had just died at Sykion in the Peloponnesos, Antony married Octavian's sister Octavia as a surety of peace and alliance with his former adversary. From that time on, the preceding winter at Alexandria could have seemed like a mere affair, an inconsequential episode.

At that very time, Cleopatra gave birth to twins, a boy and a girl, whom she named Alexander Helios and Cleopatra Selene,[41] children whose paternity Antony later acknowledged. This twin birth was a good omen, and the surnames they were given (Sun and Moon) proclaimed the divine nature of the idyll of which they were the fruit. Dazzling though it was, this union seemed to have been short-lived, for the news from Italy left scarcely any hope of an early return of the triumvir to Alexandria. In fact, Antony and Cleopatra would be separated for three and a half years, from the spring of 40 to the fall of 37, and during this period Cleopatra practically disappeared from history, according to the principle that Roman affairs were the sole subject of interest to our sources.

A single author, Flavius Josephus, makes a passing allusion to Cleopatra during the absence of Antony. Herod, who was administering the Jewish state along with his brother Phasaël in the name of the high priest Hyrkanos II, had managed to escape the Parthians when they invaded Palestine in 41–40. Quite naturally, he fled to Egypt. When he arrived at Pelusium, Egyptian ships escorted him to Alexandria, where Cleopatra bade him to remain, even offering him the command of an army that she proposed to send on expedition.[42] Herod declined the offer and left for Rhodes, later proceeding to Rome. The anecdote, which is undoubtedly drawn from the personal *Memoirs* of the future king Herod, must be authentic: More than a century earlier, Cleopatra's predecessors had entrusted such commands to Jewish officers, so great was their reputation. Furthermore, Herod had already distinguished himself in Palestine with his military talents. We must therefore understand that after Antony's departure for Italy, Cleopatra was thinking of launching Egypt into the war against the Parthians. The unrealistic character of such an enterprise and the Parthians' lack of hostility toward the Lagide kingdom doubtless led to abandonment of the plan. Still, the queen must have regretted having allowed her guest to leave. In fact, the latter managed to obtain from the senate, in recognition of his fidelity to Rome, the title King of the Jews, with the support of Antony himself, who viewed him as a key player in the reconquest of the East.[43] Of no great significance at the time, Herod's promotion would prove to make him a major obstacle to the queen's ambitions.

Excluded from the political game in Rome, did Cleopatra use the services of the Egyptian astrologer attached to Antony's retinue to cause a falling out with Octavian and a breakup with Octavia?[44] If such was the case, the efforts of the magus scarcely succeeded, at least on the second point, for when Antony returned to the East in the fall of 39, he settled in Athens, accompanied by his wife, who had just given him a daughter, Antonia. From Athens, Antony prepared the liberation of the Roman provinces and the allied territories of Asia occupied by the Parthians. But instead of directing the operations himself, he entrusted them to his loyal deputy, Publius Ventidius, a gifted officer who owed his remarkable social advancement to Caesar. Ventidius defeated Labienus in Asia Minor, and then, not far from Antioch, the crown prince Pakoros, who died in combat on June 9, 38. For the first time in its history, Rome prevailed over the Parthians. Antony intervened personally only to crush Antiochos of Commagene, one of the kings who had abandoned the alliance with Rome. The latter was forced to hand over his capital, Samosata, on the banks of the Euphrates.

But the victory, which was consecrated by a triumph celebrated at Rome by Ventidius, was a precarious one, for despite its reverses, Parthian power remained intact. Further, many eastern territories, whose people and local leaders had long since grown impatient with the rapacity of the representatives of Rome, were always ready to side with the latter's enemies. Antony was thus obliged to contemplate an entirely different campaign, which he needed to conduct in person to assure the future security of the Mediterranean East. To do so, he had to assure himself once again of the cooperation of the West—in this case, of Octavian. The latter had just experienced serious reversals in his struggle with Sextus Pompey, the last of the sons of the great Pompey, who was maintaining his hold on Sicily and threatening the provisioning of Rome with his mastery of the sea. In the treaty of Tarentum in 37, Antony exchanged 120 ships Octavian needed to eliminate Sextus Pompey for 20,000 legionaries for the coming Parthian war; moreover, the triumvirate, which had officially expired at the end of 38, was renewed for five years.

The Resurrection of the Lagide Empire

In the fall of 37, Antony left Italy for the last time. Octavia, who had accompanied him as far as Corfu, was asked to return to Rome, where she would give birth to a second daughter, Antonia the younger. Meanwhile, Antony made his way toward Antioch. This city, one of the largest in the East, was ideally situated to carry out the political reorganization of the territories won back from the Parthians, as well as the military preparations for the great expedition that was planned for the following spring. One of Antony's first acts was to invite Cleopatra to join him, as he had done at Tarsos in 41, though the context of this new summons was quite different. Whatever the pretext for sending Octavia back to Italy, it was bound to seem like a repudiation of his legitimate wife for the purpose of taking up again with the queen of Egypt, as though such a long separation had only increased the passion that Antony felt for her.

Of course, motives other than passionate feelings could have justified the reunion. The support of Egypt was essential to the new project of a war against Parthia; moreover, the presence of the queen was required for the redistribution of territories that Antony considered indispensable for the new policy that he intended to conduct in the East in the name of Rome. The various generals (Lucullus, Pompey, Caesar) who had succeeded one another in the region over a span of thirty years had each attempted to resolve the complex problems posed by the political organization of a multicultural and multiethnic East to guarantee both stability and submission to Rome. After the failures of the schemes that had been devised by his predecessors, Antony decided to minimize direct administration by Roman representatives and to augment the role of the allied states, on the condition of entrusting the latter to loyal rulers.

Thus, most of Asia Minor was divided among three new kings who, since they did not belong to any established dynasty, owed their elevation solely to the favor of the triumvir: in Galatia, Amyntas, former secretary of a fallen petty king; in Pontos, Polemon, son of a local politician; and in Cappadocia, Archelaos, who bore the same name as his father, Cleopatra's ephemeral brother-in-law,[45] and whose mother had been one of Antony's mistresses. Finally, in Palestine, Herod had just been installed in his new kingdom of Judea by Gaius Sosius, one of Antony's loyal lieutenants. But the originality of the system put in place at this time was revealed in the concessions accorded to Cleopatra: Not only was she confirmed in her possession of Cyprus, but she also received a number of cities and territories on the Syro-Palestinian coast and in Cilicia. Among these, she was even able to annex an entire state, the Arab kingdom of Chalkis, whose sovereign had collaborated with the Parthians.[46]

Thus, with no resistance, Cleopatra had reconstituted in large part the Lagide empire of her forebears, which had dominated the Mediterranean world in the third century. The material and moral advantages she obtained were so great that at this time, the queen inaugurated a new era marked by a second numbering of her regnal years.[47] But this expansion was not the fruit of a policy of conquest; it was due only to the privileged relations that the queen had established with one of the leaders of the only world power at that time. To preserve and even to extend an edifice built on such a fragile foundation, Cleopatra thus depended both on the influence she could exercise on her benefactor and on the maintenance of the latter's dominant position on the Roman political chessboard.

Contrary to appearances, Antony's position in no way implied an abandonment of Roman interests to the sole advantage of the Egyptian sovereign. The evidently exorbitant privileges he had granted to her could be interpreted as elements of a coherent policy on the part of a representative of Rome, and it was thus that they were understood in the West, where they aroused some murmurs, but scarcely any protests. After all, had not Antony maintained and even strengthened the three key provinces of the Roman East—Asia, Bithynia, and Syria? And had he not supported Herod against the demands of the queen, who was casting a covetous eye on the kingdom of Judea, the last territorial obstacle between Egypt and its new possessions in Syria? People thus could only wait to see what would follow.

The Campaign in the East

The winter of 37–36 spent by the two lovers at Antioch must have seemed like a repetition of the one they had experienced four years earlier at Alexandria, and we can imagine that the association of the "Inimitables" was resuscitated for the occasion. But on this occasion, Antony did not remain idle; rather, he devoted himself to putting together a formidable fighting machine numbering 100,000 men, of which 30,000 were furnished by the allies. Circumstances seemed favorable, for the situation at the Parthian court was in utter confusion: King Orodes II, who had vanquished Crassus, had just been assassinated by his younger brother, Phraates IV. In reaction, a whole party of high dignitaries, led by a certain Monaises, had gone over to the Roman side. The objective of the campaign was the submission of the Parthian power and its allies. The strategy was audacious: It consisted of a vast flanking movement intended to catch the heart of the enemy empire from the rear, in the process crossing through Armenia, which had previously been brought to heel, and then the kingdom of Media, which was to be reduced along the way.

Alas! Antony, who dreamed of repeating Alexander's exploits against the Persian empire, was instead the distant precursor of Napoleon and his campaign in Russia. Bad luck, tactical errors, and acts of treason transformed his triumphant advance into a debacle that was later unjustly imputed to the general's amorous obsession with his Egyptian mistress.[48] In October, after persisting in maintaining a futile siege before the Median capital, Antony was forced to retreat in order to avoid being caught in the trap of winter. The return to Syria across the mountains of Media and Armenia was a thorough disaster for a worn and starving army incessantly harassed by an unpredictable enemy. Admirable in adversity, Antony barely avoided annihilation, thanks to his courage and his charisma. His losses amounted to more than 32,000 men, nearly half the Roman troops. The survivors were in pitiful condition, and Antony needed urgently to find money, clothing, and provisions in order to prevent desertions. From Leukè Kômè (White Village), an obscure little port on the Phoenician coast between Beirut and Sidon, he sent out a call for assistance to Cleopatra, who had returned to Alexandria when the expedition departed. The latter delayed, more likely because of difficulties in collecting and shipping the relief that Antony requested than out of bad faith, as her enemies claimed. The defeated triumvir took to drinking while he awaited her. When Cleopatra finally appeared, he had at least the consolation of seeing the latest child she had given him, Ptolemy Philadelphos.

While Antony was experiencing this disastrous setback, Octavian was enjoying unhoped-for successes in the West, to the point of being able to declare an end to the civil wars. The indomitable Sextus Pompey had finally been crushed in a naval engagement at Cape Naulochus on September 3, 36, by Agrippa, who was by far the most brilliant of Octavian's generals. Lepidus, the third triumvir, had thought he could profit from the situation to add Sicily to his African domain. This was an inept and presumptuous move, for Octavian, being in the net position of force, made it a pretext for deposing Lepidus from power. The triumvirate, which had been extended at Tarentum in 37, was reduced to a de facto duumvirate, a circumstance that could justly cause Antony to worry.

Octavian, however, did not want to seem to be exploiting the situation for his own profit. Undoubtedly because of the intervention of Octavia, admirably faithful to her adulterous husband, he allowed the same honors to be paid to both himself and Antony, as though the Median campaign had been a victory for the Roman people. Further, he feigned complaisance to the point of sending assistance to his colleague so that he could complete his glorious war against the Parthians. In doing so, Octavian was in fact beginning the tortuous propaganda efforts that would ultimately enable him to gain victory over his adversary. While attracting general approbation for his cooperation with Antony in the public interest, he succeeded in transforming this cooperation into a veritable poisoned chalice. The assistance consisted essentially of seventy ships, which Antony did not need for a theater of operations that was entirely landlocked. This squadron was in any case merely the remnant of the navy of 120 ships that Antony had furnished for the war against Sextus Pompey. The two thousand legionaries whom Octavian also granted him represented only a tenth of the contingent he had promised in exchange for the vessels at the time of the accords of Tarentum in 37, but which he had never sent. Finally—the ultimate treachery—the conducting of the detachment was personally entrusted to Octavia, who was anxious to rejoin a husband whose infidelity seemed to her to be remediable. She soon made her appearance at Athens, accompanied by the troops and the ships.

Antony's Revenge

We can imagine the discomfiture that seized the two lovers when Octavia's approach was announced in the spring of 35. Cleopatra feared that Antony, touched by the devotion of his legitimate wife and desirous of avoiding irremediable discord with Octavian, might choose to rejoin Octavia. Did Cleopatra employ all the artifices described by Plutarch to dissuade Antony from joining Octavia,[49] or were those only the inventions of the hostile propaganda directed against the queen? Antony likely had already wagered everything on the East. Further, he could not resume living with his wife without at the same stroke recognizing the preeminence of his brother-in-law. He saw himself as the second Alexander, and not as second in command of Octavian's empire. He had no future except with Cleopatra.

As a result, Octavia quickly received a message from her husband telling her to turn back and to send him the reinforcements she had led that far. This reaction was undoubtedly what Octavian had counted on. Octavia's return caused consternation among even the most fervent of the many partisans Antony still had at Rome, all the more so in that Octavia further stirred up emotions by abstaining from any recrimination. She even continued to live in the house of her adulterous husband and to treat the children he had had with Fulvia like her own.

While Antony, now resident once more at Alexandria, was recovering from his setback and preparing his revenge on the Parthians, Octavian embarked with success on a war against the Illyrian tribes who were threatening the Roman positions on the Adriatic coast. Above all, this was a good pretext for exercising his troops, a prelude to a future confrontation with the East. On his return, instead of celebrating a triumph, he had exceptional honors awarded to his sister Octavia and his wife, Livia,[50] thus contrasting the merits of women such as these to the supposed vices of Cleopatra, which would become one of the favorite themes of his propaganda.

Antony, for his part, had to resolve the question of Pompey. After his Sicilian defeat, Sextus Pompey had in fact proceeded to Asia Minor, where he raised a small army. Cleopatra was of the opinion that this indomitable personage and brilliant general could be an important advantage in the coming conflict between the two triumvirs, which she also believed was inevitable,[51] and Antony was prepared to rally to her views, despite the declaration of hostility that such an alliance would have immediately signified for Octavian. But Sextus, after Antony's setback in Media, had made a foolish attempt at an agreement with the Parthians, thus repeating the conduct of the republican Labienus five years earlier. It was difficult to pardon such treason, and Antony thus dispatched an army that defeated and captured Sextus. The latter was put to death, perhaps without Antony's consent. Octavian's propaganda, however, later had him bear the responsibility, as though it had been an act of gratuitous cruelty, and contrasted it to the *clementia* of Antony's opponent, of which Lepidus had been the beneficiary under nearly the same circumstances.

Meanwhile, unexpected news arrived at Alexandria. The king of the Medes was quarreling with the Parthian king Phraates IV over the division of the spoils left behind by the Roman army during the previous expedition. The former was now ready to switch allegiance and even to support the Romans in a future campaign against his erstwhile suzerain. Assuring the willing co-operation of Armenia thus became the key to avoiding any risk of a fresh disaster, for the ambiguous attitude of the Armenian sovereign had played a significant role in the debacle of 36. To strengthen ties with Armenia, Antony proposed a marriage be-tween the first son he had had with Cleopatra and the daughter of its king.[52] Thus pressured to rally openly to the Roman cause, the king proved his hostility by declining to respond; Antony, who had in the meantime mobilized a new army, marched on Artaxata, the Armenian capital, in the spring of 34. On this occa-sion, Cleopatra accompanied him as far as the Euphrates.[53] On her return journey, she stopped in Judea, where Herod received her with overblown magnificence. Even so, a serious bone of contention divided the two sovereigns. Cleopatra had never ac-cepted the resurrection of the Jewish kingdom to the profit of the Idumaean, and she had employed all sorts of pretexts to get Antony to depose the latter, while exploiting, in obscure in-trigues, the friendship that linked her to Alexandra, the king's mother-in-law. Until then, Cleopatra had succeeded only in de-spoiling Herod of the revenues of the fruitful groves of balsam and palm trees in the environs of Jericho. According to Flavius Josephus, she now attempted to seduce her enemy, with the design of later denouncing him to Antony. In no way duped by such advances, Herod renounced his foolhardy intention of assassinating the queen only upon the exhortations of his friends. This story, evidently drawn from the personal memoirs of the Jewish king, reeks too much of self-justification for us to accord it credulity.

For his part, Antony had forced the Armenian King Artabazes to negotiate. Though the latter's son then seized the throne with the support of the nobility, the Roman legions quickly broke the Armenian resistance and forced the usurper to flee to the Parthians. Impressed by the demonstration of force in this neighboring land, the Median king agreed to the betrothal of his only daughter to Antony's son.[54] Artabazes was brought in chains of silver to Alexandria as living proof of a brilliant victory.

"Queen of Kings Whose Sons Are Kings"

While this campaign was a brilliant success, its objective had been far more modest than that of the preceding expedition. The subjection of Armenia, a secondary power, could only be a pale substitute for bringing the immense Parthian empire to heel, though Antony surely hoped that the campaign might be the prelude to the latter. Nevertheless, he decided to give his success a particular luster. In the fall of 34, Alexandria was the theater of an extraordinary spectacle that even today plunges historians into the depths of perplexity. This would have been a good opportunity for Antony to celebrate his exploits in Armenia with a triumph at Rome. Instead, he marched his troops in the Egyptian capital, preceded by captives, including Artabazes, who now wore chains of gold. Seated on a throne that was also of gold,

The remainder of the East was thus theoretically attached to a composite empire directed, in the last instance, by Cleopatra. We can easily imagine the difficulties in assessing this spectacle, the propaganda of the one camp and the other, and the actual political intentions behind this manifest insanity. The authors who report the episode, Plutarch[56] and Dio Cassius,[57] give us a view distorted by Augustan propaganda, with an implicit stress on the "treason" of an Antony subjugated by Cleopatra. In reality, this Ceremony of the Donations at Alexandria had only the effect of a proclamation with no immediate consequences for the political organization of the East. Among other obstacles, the age of the beneficiaries—six and two—stood in the way of effective control over the regions handed over to them, a good part of which, moreover, were outside the control of Antony. As for Cleopatra, not only was her own domain not extended beyond the enlargements already granted to her three years earlier, but she was obliged, in theory, to lose territories ceded to Antony's children, such as Cyrenaica to Selene and Cilicia to Philadelphos.

The issues of coinage illustrate most accurately the meaning of this new policy defined at Alexandria. On the denarii of Roman standard, the portrait and the name of Antony are accompanied by the legend ARMENIA DEVICTA celebrating the victory over Armenia in 34, while on the reverse, Cleopatra is depicted as "Queen of Kings whose sons are kings."[58] Other silver coins, of the Greek standard (tetradrachms), also associated Antony, designated as triumvir, with Cleopatra, "Queen and Youngest Goddess."[59] While the definition of Antony's powers did not transgress Roman legality, that of Cleopatra's royalty conformed to the Hellenistic ideology of the divine monarch—but it was Antony alone who controlled the military force invoked by the commemoration of the victory over Armenia. What was taking shape was the concept of an East governed by kings according to their own customs rather than subjected to the arbitrary power of proconsuls, on condition that Rome maintained the power of arms and the supreme right of arbitration. The solidarity of such a partnership would be guaranteed by the mixed origin of these kings, issued from a carnal alliance between the last representative of the former dynasties, Cleopatra, and the successive masters of the Roman empire, Caesar and Antony. The Roman people, in return, would reap the fruits of a prosperity engendered by peace.

Cleopatra, Enemy of Rome

Toward the Rupture with Octavian

Whether or not such an ideological project underlay the proclamations in Alexandria, they could scarcely have been well received in Rome. Many of Antony's supporters, consternated and alarmed at the possible effects of such a manifesto on Roman public opinion, at first avoided any excess of public discussion of Antony's initiatives, as did Octavian himself (Figures 5 and 6), who feared that his adversary's Armenian victory would eclipse his own successes in Illyria. The two camps exchanged increasingly hostile official messages and letters in which the triumvirs heaped reproaches on each other.[1] The liaison with Cleopatra was not the only target of Octavian's attacks, for he was much more deeply shocked by the recognition of Caesarion as a legitimate son of Caesar, implying that he himself was not the dictator's sole heir. Other accusations were more artificial or stamped with utter bad faith, such as that concerning the murder of Sextus Pompey or the supposedly unworthy treatment of the Armenian king. Antony, for his part, reproached Octavian for having sent him only meager reinforcements in the war against the Parthians, for having seized the territories and the troops of Sextus Pompey and Lepidus without having granted him anything,

Figure 5. Silver denarius depicting the goddess Victoria (above) and Octavian (the future Augustus) riding in a triumphal quadriga. From the Ottilia Buerger Collection of Ancient and Byzantine Coins. Photo courtesy of Lawrence University, Appleton, Wisconsin.

and finally, for having distributed all available Italian land to his own veterans to the detriment of those of the armies of the East. To these charges he added purely private grievances vented in sometimes trivial missives, such as that cited by Suetonius in which Antony, after conceding that he was sleeping with the queen, included a highly instructive list of Octavian's mistresses.[2]

This war of words was accompanied by fairly adroit maneu-

Figure 6. Gold aureus depicting Augustus (above) and the goddess Diana. From the Ottilia Buerger Collection of Ancient and Byzantine Coins. Photo courtesy of Lawrence University, Appleton, Wisconsin.

vers, as the two adversaries assaulted each other behind a legalistic façade and with feigned moderation in the hope of attracting a majority of senators. Thus, Antony proposed to lay down his powers as triumvir if Octavian would agree to do the same—and thus to restore the republic—knowing full well that the latter would refuse and at the same stroke alienate Roman opinion.

While Antony was leading a new campaign, or rather a military promenade, to the boundaries of Media to reinforce his recent alliance with the king of that country, he received a message from Octavian that left no doubt that a rupture was imminent. He then decided to prepare for war, and with this objective, to concentrate his forces at Ephesos, where Cleopatra soon joined him, bringing two hundred ships, large quantities of provisions, and a considerable sum of money.[3]

In the Roman senate, tension reached its height in January 32. The two consuls who assumed office in that month were well-known partisans of Antony, who counted on them to uphold his cause and to make difficulties for his adversary. They failed in their attempts, however, for Octavian intimidated the senate with menacing words and the deployment of force. Without waiting for the inevitable counterattack, the consuls fled to Antony's camp with more than two hundred senators. The quarrel between the two colleagues thus grew into a schism within the very bosom of the venerable governing institution of the Roman republic. Like Pompey in 49, Antony now had his own senate and his own magistrates, but neither of the two camps as yet wished to initiate an armed conflict. Octavian even pretended that the departure of the consuls and a portion of the senate had his blessings, declining to view it as a *casus belli*. In fact, he was experiencing extreme difficulties raising the troops he needed and putting together a fleet capable of opposing that of Antony.

Antony's official repudiation of Octavia, expelling her from his house at Rome, where she had persisted in residing until then, was also not a pretext for a declaration of war.[4] For Cleopatra, this long-deferred divorce was a victory that definitively linked Antony's destiny to her own, though the unofficial status of their union remained unchanged. The rupture of this final tie between the triumvirs led Octavian to pull out all the stops with regard to propaganda. With no regard for the illegality or even the sacrilege of such an act, he had the testament that Antony had entrusted to the Vestals forcibly seized in order to make it public. The provision that aroused the greatest indignation concerned the place that Antony had designated for his burial: He chose to rest at Alexandria, next to Cleopatra![5] Octavian fed the scandal with a well-orchestrated campaign, aided by defectors from the enemy camp, spreading actual and supposed facts illustrating intentions imputed to Antony of subjecting Rome to Alexandria and its queen. The latter was identified with Omphale, the mythic queen of the Lydians who had reduced Herakles to bondage and forced him to dress and act like a woman.[6] It was precisely Herakles whom Antony claimed as his ancestor and model. Such insinuations were the best means of inducing the Romans and all of Italy to accept the extreme sacrifices Octavian was demanding in order to put together his army and his fleet.

All this propaganda ill concealed Octavian's weakness, while Antony could dispose of five hundred warships and thirty well-equipped legions, to which were added 25,000 auxiliary infantry and 12,000 cavalry. To finance such a concentration of forces, Antony issued an unprecedented number of coins that flooded the entire East, circulating everywhere the image of his eagles and his vessels and the name of each of his army corps.[7]

We can easily believe, with Plutarch, that with such a deployment, Antony could easily have won had he attacked Italy in this summer of 32, when his adversary was still vulnerable. His partisans, who had not yet left Rome and who were obliged to hide their sentiments in the face of the ever more hysterical propaganda spread by Octavian's minions, believed that he had only to make his appearance to rally all of the undecideds and malcontents and thus, without resistance, to overturn an unpopular regime—on the sole condition that he rid himself of Cleopatra to quell the rumors concerning his anti-Roman intentions. They secretly dispatched an agent to convince him to act thus, but the agent was quickly found out and neutralized by the queen.[8] In fact, many of Antony's close collaborators, such as the consul Domitius Ahenobarbus, were also begging him to send Cleopatra back to Egypt, arguing that her presence lent support to Octavian's accusations and prejudiced his cause. Antony almost gave in to their entreaties, but his chief of staff, Canidius Crassus, objected that depriving himself of an ally who had furnished so large a contribution of ships, crews, and cash would damage the cohesion of military operations.[9]

The War

In the spring of 32, the lovers journeyed from Ephesos, where they had spent the winter, to the nearby island of Samos, where they organized a festival of theater and music that saw the participation of all the artists belonging to the Dionysiac guilds of Greece and Asia. Thus, while the West endured hardships imposed by Octavian's burdensome military preparations, joy and opulence were the lot of the East—or at least such was the reply of Antony and Cleopatra, who meant to contrast the revelry with the heinous attacks of which they were the target. Above all, these festivities were an occasion to demonstrate the loyalty of cities and peoples to their cause. This sacred union was brilliantly embodied in the distinguished retinue of princes and kings who formed the entourage of these new masters of the East; these allies would, however, defect at the first reversals of fortune.[10]

Crossing the Aegean Sea, Antony and Cleopatra chose to reside in Athens during the summer of 32. By means of her largesse, the queen succeeded in obliterating the memory that her rival Octavia had left in this city, to the point that the Athenians, never shy of sycophantic attention, set up statues of her and Antony, both of them ranked among the gods, on the Acropolis.[11] Finally, in the autumn, they established their general quarters at Patras, in the north of the Peloponnesos. This choice indicated that the theater of operations would once again be Greece, a terrain that had scarcely proved propitious for the Pompeians in 48, or for the republicans in 42. The purely defensive strategy that Antony finally adopted proved to be a major error. Limited to a line of fortified sites on the western coast of Greece from Corfu to Cape Tainaron, the arrangement was intended to protect the maritime route to Egypt; however, the fragility of that strategy would soon be revealed.

At just that time, Octavian felt he was at last ready for the final confrontation and decided to take the plunge. The moment was propitious, for the rule of the triumvirate, which had been extended for five years in 37, would legally expire at the end of 32. He could thus deprive Antony of all his powers without infringing the law. Further, not wishing to be held responsible for a fresh civil war after having declared an end to such wars five years earlier, he presented the situation as a conflict with a foreign power. To this end, he respected the letter of all the ancestral rituals that obligatorily surrounded every declaration of war. The designated enemy was Cleopatra, and she alone. The pretext was the intention imputed to the queen of Egypt of reducing Rome to slavery, as she had already done with Antony. Was she not swearing that she would one day personally dispense justice from the height of the Capitoline?[12] In thus naming only Cleopatra as the one at fault, Octavian pretended to offer Antony a way out: He had only to abandon the cause of the Egyptian queen to regain his place in Roman political life. His partisans could in any case benefit from this same immunity, as many of them did once the tide turned.

The hostilities that finally ensued would last only two seasons before Octavian won his definitive victory. Yet it was not he who proved to be the principal architect of his triumph, but rather his loyal friend Agrippa, one of the most brilliant tacticians of antiquity. He was able in particular to take advantage of Antony's indecisiveness and of the inertia that was the principal cause of the latter's loss. The capture of Methone in early spring 31 threatened Antony's positions and the supply route from Egypt. After easily taking Corfu in the north, Octavian had no difficulty in landing his troops and systematically occupying the coast and the islands as he made his way toward the Ambracian Gulf, where the main contingent of Antony's fleet had cast anchor. Accompanied by Cleopatra, Antony hastened from Patras and encamped on the southern coast of the straits that gave access to the gulf, near the famous temple of Apollo at Actium. For several months, the two enemies remained face to face there, repeatedly attacking each other without either of them succeeding in gaining the advantage. While Antony exhausted his forces trying unsuccessfully to dislodge Octavian, and while ever more numerous defectors sapped the morale of his camp, Agrippa captured most of his base camps, the island of Leukas, and in particular Patras, his general quarters, rendering his situation untenable. Instead of abandoning his ships, which were now useless, and forcing the enemy into a battle on land, as his chief of staff advised, Antony chose to run the blockade, thus siding with Cleopatra, who could not bring herself to scuttle her fleet.

Augustan propaganda stigmatized the queen's conduct on the fatal day of September 2, 31: She deliberately betrayed her ally by making off toward the Peloponnesos with her sixty ships, while Antony, dumbfounded and wild with passion, was constrained to abandon his own ships to follow her.[13] In reality, the battle had been lost before it began, given the superiority of the positions that Octavian held. The safety of the flower of the squadron and of the Lagide treasure on board could well have been one of Antony's objectives, but he committed a serious tactical error in suddenly leaving the combat that was raging in his haste to join the queen's ship. Scarcely more than sixty vessels out of a total of

lovers, who had undoubtedly had no relations since Actium, soon found themselves in the bosom of a new club in which the former "Inimitables" gallantly styled themselves "Those Who Will Die Together" (*synapothanoumenoi*);[17] and the feasts began again. . . .

If Octavian spent nearly an entire year putting the finishing touches on his victory, the cause was not the resistance of Antony's party, but rather the tensions within his own camp. He was thus obliged to return to Italy to manage various crises, including a revolt of his own veterans, who were discontent with their lot. He needed to cope with a lack of cash, and the simplest solution was to seize the Lagide treasure. Fear that the latter might escape him caused him to proceed, though with caution, to capture Egypt. He ordered Cornelius Gallus, who had replaced Scarpus at Cyrene, to invade the land from the Libyan side. Antony met him at Paraitonion but was unable to prevent him from capturing the place and continuing his eastward advance. Meanwhile, Octavian advanced along the Syrian coast, reaching Ptolemais, the future Saint John of Acre, where he was magnificently received by Herod, who had not feared, as a clever politician, to meet him previously at Rhodes to convince him of the sincerity of his allegiance. Cleopatra's prejudices against the king whom Antony had given to the Jews thus found their bitter confirmation.

Around this time, many obscure negotiations occurred between the two camps. Plutarch and especially Dio Cassius insinuate that Cleopatra played a double game, trying to negotiate without Antony's knowledge and to his displeasure.[18] It is unlikely, however, that the queen would have so easily allowed herself to be deceived by the ridiculous amorous advances that Dio attributes to Octavian, though the role of Thyrsos, a young emissary he sent to Cleopatra, remains mysterious.[19] Separating fact from rumor and legend in these final negotiations is a challenge. Nevertheless, it is probable that the queen attempted to persuade Octavian to spare her children, and perhaps even to permit Caesarion to reign over an Egypt that was once again a vassal of Rome. The only thing she could have offered him in return was free access to Egypt and its capital. Did she, in this situation, agree to deliver the fortified town of Pelusium, the key to Egypt, without a fight in exchange for some vague promises?[20] Such was the rumor that soon spread, but again, the naiveté of such conduct is scarcely compatible with what we otherwise know regarding her character. She had no reason to believe the conciliatory messages that Octavian was sending her. In fact, she lent them so little credence that well before the arrival of the enemy legions, she arranged for Caesarion to flee to the Meroitic kingdom in the Sudan.[21] She, for her part, shut herself up with her treasure and some servants in the tomb she had built for herself, proof that she did not wish to fall into the hands of the victor alive. Meanwhile, Antony attempted to mobilize the remnant of his land and sea forces for a hopeless resistance.

The End

This last stand, in the year 30, was followed by the final defections. On August 1 (of the Roman calendar then in use, corresponding to August 3 of our own),[22] Octavian's troops made their way into Alexandria via the Canopic gate, through which a mysterious Dionysiac procession had exited the preceding night, symbolizing the withdrawal of Antony's tutelary god and of the Lagide dynasty. Thanks to Plutarch[23] and Dio Cassius,[24] who drew their information from the memoirs of the queen's personal physician, no detail of the tragic sequence of events has escaped us, from the suicide of Antony, who was deceived by false news of Cleopatra's death, down to the latter's end some nine days later. Here, we shall confine ourselves to an enumeration of the principal events: the dying Antony hauled up by ropes into the mausoleum, where he expired in the queen's arms; the stratagem that enabled Octavian's emissary to prevent the destruction by fire of the royal treasure and to capture Cleopatra alive; the illness she herself contracted after Antony's funeral; her dramatic interview with the man who had defeated her; and finally, her suicide in the company of her two faithful servants. The body of the queen was discovered recumbent on a golden bed, sumptuously adorned and clutching the insignia of her ancestors, both pharaonic and Macedonian. Conscious of her image to the end, she insisted on surrounding her death with the grandeur she had displayed throughout her life, compelling her enemies to recognize in her the dignity of "a queen issued from so many kings," as her lady-in-waiting Charmion described her to the soldiers who discovered the scene, just before she, too, died.

The general framework of the facts is not in doubt, despite notable discrepancies between the two principal versions. Despite the integrity of that framework, however, a number of problems remain. Did Octavian really intend to display Cleopatra in his triumph at Rome, and did he employ all sorts of measures to keep her alive for this reason? This is what our two principal narrators seem to maintain. Yet in Plutarch, the intervention of Cornelius Dolabella,[25] who revealed his patron's intentions in this regard and thus precipitated the queen's fatal decision, would seem to mask a Machiavellian tactic on Octavian's part. While the latter could not, on his own initiative, deprive the Roman people of the finest ornament of his triumph, he had much to fear from the negative effects of the spectacle of this woman in chains. For more than two years, she had been the target of a frenzied campaign intended to arouse an almost irrational hatred of her. Yet the effects of this campaign could be undone: Had this "dire monster"[26] forged by his propaganda made an appearance, hostil-

73

ity might have been transformed into compassion. Would Octavian have made the same error as that committed by his adoptive father when the latter thought he could satisfy the voyeurism of the *plebs* by making a display of Arsinoe, Cleopatra's own sister? For the victor at Actium to remain the "savior of the liberty of the Roman People,"[27] the enemy of that liberty could make no appearance at Rome.

The circumstances of Cleopatra's suicide—the apparent ease of the act and the method used—remain mysterious. The ease of the suicide suggests Octavian's tacit complicity, though he convinced posterity of the opposite. In fact, not the least of his ideological *tours de force* was his transformation of such an act, which in his own time was normally considered noble and courageous, into an ultimate treachery on the part of the queen, who thus deprived him of the opportunity to display his famous *clementia*.

The method of the suicide plunged the ancients into perplexity. Though he was a contemporary of the events, even Strabo was wary of choosing between two contradictory versions, one attributing the queen's death to poison, the other entailing serpents.[28] We find the same reserve in Plutarch[29] and Dio Cassius.[30] But the theory of one or more serpents soon prevailed, notwithstanding its manifest unlikelihood. Thus, the official poets of the Augustan era—Virgil, Horace, and Propertius—all evoke deadly serpents. Such a death had the power to strike the imagination with its many symbolic and religious implications. The rumor was fed by the fact that in the triumphal procession at Rome, there was a statue depicting a queen with an asp around her arm. This was not Cleopatra, however, but rather a representation of Isis holding a serpent in her role as magician.[31] With such an iconographic basis, we can understand how the legend of the asp gained precedence, to the point of becoming an indisputable fact. Modern scholars have taken up the tradition, finding many meanings in this supposed viper (which would rather have been a cobra), some having to do with Hellenistic beliefs and others derived from ancient pharaonic cults.[32] It is certainly difficult to believe that the queen would have chosen such an uncomfortable means of death merely to satisfy the interpretive frenzies of posterity!

The Epilogue

Thus, on August 12, 30, the last queen of Egypt put an end to her life, no doubt by poisoning herself, in the company of her two servants, Iras and Charmion.[33] Secretly relieved, Octavian accorded her a royal funeral and had her remains placed next to those of Antony. He then waited for the change of year in the Egyptian calendar (which at that time corresponded to August 30) to inaugurate a new era in the land of the Nile. For him, there was no question of leaving Egypt to the queen's children, either Caesarion or those of Antony. The former was put to death, and the latter were entrusted to Octavia. Cleopatra Selene had the good fortune of marrying the Numidian prince Juba, and thus of becoming queen of Mauritania, and giving birth to a son, the last of the Ptolemies, who by an irony of fate was assassinated by his own cousin, Caligula. We do not know what became of Cleopatra's other children, Alexander Helios and Ptolemy Philadelphos, whose education Octavia was supposed to assure.

While the population of Alexandria was spared, the entourage of Cleopatra and Antony earned an unequal treatment. Though imbued with remarkable clemency, the victor could display ferocity toward Romans who had ignored all opportunities to change sides, but whose apparent loyalty to Antony often stemmed only from irreversible past commitments. This was the case with Caesar's last living assassin, Cassius of Parma. Canidius Crassus also perished, along with Quintus Ovinius,[34] a senator

75

who had managed the royal wool-knitting establishments and who must thus have furnished the uniforms worn by Antony's legions. The Alexandrian Sophist Philostratos, a smooth talker and embroiderer of fact who had profited from Cleopatra's penchant for philosophy to become one of her intimates, was saved from probable execution by his colleague and compatriot Areios, who had long since emigrated to Rome and acquired the same position in the retinue of the young Caesar.[35]

Though Octavian insisted on paying homage before the remains of Alexander, no doubt searching for some sign of approbation in the mummified visage of the Conqueror, he refused to visit the tombs of the Ptolemies, mere inglorious cadavers, or to venerate the Apis bull, which the priests wished to introduce to him.[36] Octavian thus declined to be successor to the Lagides and their faded pharaonic finery, demonstrating how he differed from an Antony ready to reject his Roman heritage for the mirages of the East. Egypt, which he had conquered, like Alexander, at the point of a lance, was added to the empire of the Roman people; but, wary of the power it could bestow on the one who governed it, he in fact treated it as his private domain. Despite his initial attitude, his power at Rome approached that of an absolute monarch, and the Egyptian priests soon invested him with all the attributes of the pharaoh he had disdained to become.

Conclusion: The Memory of Cleopatra

The natural opportunism of the clergy did not lead it to forget the last of its queens, whose cult would endure here and there in Egypt, though on a modest scale. One of Cleopatra's favorite clerics, a certain Archibios, sought to keep her statues from being toppled, supposedly giving Octavian the scarcely credible sum of two thousand talents to spare them.[1] Some of these must still have been standing four centuries later, for in 373 C.E., when Christianity was triumphing everywhere, a priest of Isis still boasted of having gilded an effigy of Cleopatra,[2] at that time undoubtedly believed to be a hypostasis of Isis.

In Rome, Octavian, now Augustus, was no longer interested in obliterating the memory of his enemy. All Augustan ideology was in fact based on his victory at Actium, which had officially been won over Cleopatra alone. The personality of the queen could therefore not be underestimated: The loser had to be as incomparable as the exploit, and the eulogists of the new regime, from Virgil to Horace, found material for inspiration in her. Cleopatra haunted the imagination of the Greco-Roman world: Her magnificence, her pride, her alleged lewdness, the circumstances of her death but also her learning, her magical arts, and of course the romance of her passionate loves all became common literary themes that would endure long after the reign of Augustus.

It is this tradition that is the most astonishing phenomenon.[3] Writers throughout the eras have experienced Cleopatra's personality as the incarnation of their fantasies, to the point of forging entirely contradictory representations of her. From the Middle Ages through the nineteenth century, accounts of her ranged from Boccaccio's greedy, cruel, lascivious bitch to Théophile Gauthier's veritable archetype of the ideal woman. By turns, she has been vilified as a satanic prostitute and celebrated for her wisdom and chastity. Of course, from the sixteenth century on, the romantic aspect prevailed, especially once Plutarch's text became widely available in the translation by Jacques Amyot; through the intermediary of an English version, it inspired Shakespeare's famous tragedy. The nineteenth century saw the first biographies that could be called historical, while the twentieth breathed new life into the myth through the magic of the silver screen; in the course of time, Cleopatra came to sport the visages of Claudette Colbert, Vivien Leigh, and Elizabeth Taylor.

The real Cleopatra remains elusive behind all the masks that have been put on her, and since the accounts of the ancient classical historians are themselves problematic, the only evidence beyond suspicion is the contemporary documentation. In the absence of a truth that has vanished forever, these documents, at least, transmit the image that Cleopatra herself wished to convey to her contemporaries and to posterity. Still, interpreting them correctly is essential. The funerary stela of a Buchis bull is regularly cited as evidence of the queen's interest in the native cults, but this is a thesis based on a faulty reading of the hieroglyphic text.[4] By the same token, the bas-reliefs of the divine birth sanctuary (*mammisi*) of the temple of Hermonthis in no way concern the birth of Caesarion, as has been repeated ever since Champollion.[5] But we now have a Greek papyrus, dated to 35, that gives the queen the surprising epithet Philopatris, "she who loves her country."[6] Cleopatra thus tried to express the love she felt for Egypt in a way that none of her predecessors had done. The declaration of such a relationship between the sovereign and her land, nationalistic before such a concept even existed, is an innovation we must attribute to Cleopatra.[7] With this single word, she erased centuries of foreign occupation: It was no longer a right born of the Macedonian conquest that established her royalty over Egypt, but rather a stronger attachment, a quasi-mystical bond with the land of the Nile and all who dwelled in it, whatever their origin, whose languages and beliefs she shared.

Despite that bond, Egypt is home to few contemporary vestiges of Cleopatra. Of the few native sanctuaries worked on during her reign, only the temple of Dendara is easily accessible. There, we can gaze upon an exterior wall bearing a monumental representation of the queen in her liturgical role, placed second in rank behind her son Caesarion, who is carrying out a prescribed ritual before the local gods and goddesses (Figure 7). Thus, her influence over the Egyptian people was not enough to

Figure 7. Temple of Dendara. Right: Ptolemy XV (Caesarion) and Cleopatra VII (far right) worshiping deities of the temple. Photo by Ragnhild Bjerre Finnestad.

79

convince the priests to accord her more than the place normally assigned to queens. But it is not in the temples, where pharaonic tradition took precedence over transitory political circumstances, that we must seek the true impression that Cleopatra left on her compatriots. A modest stela in the British Museum in London, inscribed in Demotic, is more revealing:[8] On January 19, 30, during the final months of Egypt's autonomy, humble weavers at Koptos were proud to designate their sovereign as "mother of kings, queen of kings, young(est) goddess." This last epithet, which the artisan confused with the expression "beneficent goddess"—nearly homonymous in the Egyptian language—is the equivalent of the title *Thea neotera* that was bestowed on Cleopatra on the occasion of her reunion with Antony in October 37. Cleopatra-Isis, divine mother of kings, eternally youthful and beneficent: Such was the memory that the Egyptian people, in the twilight of their independence, were piously prepared to preserve of the last and greatest of their queens.

Chronology of the Ptolemies

Chronology of the Ptolemies

N.B.: There is no Ptolemy VII.

Ancient Texts

An Irresistible Charm

Plutarch, "Life of Antony," 27–29

The best portrait of Cleopatra's character by an ancient historian is that by Plutarch, notwithstanding the negative preconceptions he shared with all the other authors of his time regarding the ill effects of her influence on Antony.

For her actual beauty, it is said, was not in itself so remarkable that none could be compared with her, or that no one could see her without being struck by it, but the contact of her presence, if you lived with her, was irresistible; the attraction of her person, joining with the charm of her conversation, and the character that attended all she said or did, was something bewitching. It was a pleasure merely to hear the sound of her voice, with which, like an instrument of many strings, she could pass from one language to another; so that there were few of the barbarian nations that she answered by an interpreter . . . Antony was so captivated by her that, while Fulvia his wife maintained his quarrels in Rome against Caesar by actual force of arms and the Parthian troops were . . . ready to enter Syria, he could yet suffer himself to be carried away by her to Alexandria, there to keep holiday, like a boy, in play and diversion, squandering and fooling away in enjoyments that most costly . . . of all valuables, time. They had a sort of company, to which they gave a particular name, calling it that of the Inimitable Livers. The members entertained one another daily in turn, with an extravagance of expenditure beyond measure or belief. . . .

Were Antony serious or disposed to mirth, she had at any moment some new delight or charm to meet his wishes; at every turn she was upon him, and let him escape her neither by day nor by night. She played at dice with him, drank with him, hunted with him; and when he exercised in arms, she was there to see.

E. Fuller (ed.), *Plutarch: Lives of Ten Noble Greeks and Romans* (New York, 1978): 542–45.

"Life of Antony," 53

Cleopatra, feeling her rival (i.e., Octavia) already, as it were, at hand, . . . feigned to be dying for love of Antony, bringing her body down by slender diet; when he entered the room, she fixed her eyes upon him in a rapture, and when he left, seemed to languish and half faint away. She took great pains that he should see her in tears, and, as soon as he noticed it, hastily dried them up and turned away, as if it were her wish that he should know nothing of it . . . Cleopatra's creatures were not slow to forward the design, upbraiding Antony with his unfeeling, hard-hearted temper, thus letting a woman perish whose soul depended upon him and him alone. Octavia, it was true, was his wife, and had been married to him because it was found convenient for the affairs of her brother that it should be so, and she had the honour of the title; but Cleopatra, the sovereign queen of many nations, had been contented with the name of his mistress, nor did she shun or despise the character whilst she might see him, might live with him, and enjoy him; if she were bereaved of this, she would not survive the loss. In fine, they so melted and unmanned him

that, fully believing she would die if he forsook her, he put off
the war and returned to Alexandria.

E. Fuller (ed.), *Plutarch: Lives of Ten Noble Greeks and Romans* (New
York, 1978): 572–73.

A Defeated Queen

Horace, Odes I, 37

Nunc est bibendum! *This famous verse encapsulates the relief felt by
the Romans after Octavian's victory at Actium. We note the deliberate
omission of any allusion to Antony in this poem, which was written
shortly after the death of Cleopatra. Augustan ideology is manifest
throughout this text: Responsibility for the war is placed only on the
queen of Egypt, who had been considered a drunken madwoman, but
once defeated, was viewed as a model of courage and determination in the
face of adversity.*

> At last the day has come for celebration, . . .
>
> Before today it would have been wrong to call
> For the festive Caecubean wine from the vintage bins,
> It would have been wrong while that besotted queen,
> With her vile gang of sick polluted creatures,
>
> Crazed with hope and drunk with her past successes,
> Was planning the death and destruction of the empire.
> But, comrades, she came to and sobered up
> When not one ship, almost, of all her fleet
>
> Escaped unburned, and Caesar saw to it
> That she was restored from madness to a state
> Of realistic terror. The way a hawk
> Chases a frightened dove or as a hunter
>
> Chases a hare across the snowy steppes,
> His galleys chased this fleeing queen, intending

To put the monster prodigy into chains
And bring her back to Rome. But she desired

A nobler fate than that; she did not seek
To hide her remnant fleet in a secret harbor
Nor did she, like a woman, quail with fear
At the thought of what it is that the dagger does.

She grew more fierce as she beheld her death.
Bravely, as if unmoved, she looked upon
The ruins of her palace; bravely reached out,
And touched the poison snakes, and picked them up,

And handled them, and held them to her so
Her heart might drink its fill of their black venom.
In Truth—no abject woman she—she scorned
In triumph to be brought in galleys unqueened

Across the seas to Rome to be a show.

D. Ferry (trans.), *The Odes of Horace* (New York, 1997): 97.

An Object of Hatred

Flavius Josephus, Against Apion II, 5

More than a century after her death, the memory of Cleopatra still un-leashed torrents of hatred in certain writers. This was the case with Flav-ius Josephus, heir to King Herod's former grudges, who accused the queen of anti-Semitism. She had, in fact, under circumstances that are unclear, deprived the Jews of Alexandria of a distribution of wheat, causing this indignant enumeration of other crimes committed by the queen.

Cleopatra, the last queen of Alexandria . . . indulged herself in all kinds of injustice and wicked practices, both with regard to her nearest relations and husbands who had loved her, and, in-deed, in general with regard to all the Romans, and those emper-ors that were her benefactors; who also had her sister Arsinoe slain in a temple, when she had done her no harm: moreover, she had her brother slain by private treachery, and she destroyed the gods of her country and the sepulchres of her progenitors; and while she had received her kingdom from the first Caesar, she had the impudence to rebel against his son and successor; nay, she corrupted Antony with her love-tricks, and rendered him an enemy to his country.

W. Whiston (trans.), *The Life and Works of Flavius Josephus* (Philadelphia, n.d.): 883.

The Final Days

Plutarch, "Life of Antony," 77–85

Plutarch and Dio Cassius each depicted Cleopatra's final days at length, for the most part drawing on a common source. But Dio Cassius waxed more rhetorical than his predecessor, and his account contains digressions that are exaggeratedly hostile toward the queen. Despite its many melodramatic details, Plutarch's text gives us a more credible version.

When he (i.e., Antony) understood she was still alive, he eagerly gave order to the servants to take him up, and in their arms was carried to the door of the building. Cleopatra would not open the door, but, looking from a sort of window, she let down ropes and cords, to which Antony was fastened; and she and her two women, the only persons she had allowed to enter the monument, drew him up. Those that were present say that nothing was ever more sad than this spectacle, to see Antony, covered all over with blood and just expiring, thus drawn up, still holding up his hands to her, and lifting up his body with the little force he had left. As, indeed, it was no easy task for the women; and Cleopatra, with all her force, clinging to the rope, and straining with her head to the ground, with difficulty pulled him up, while

those below encouraged her with their cries, and joined in all her
efforts and anxiety. When she had got him up, she laid him on
the bed, tearing all her clothes, which she spread upon him; and,
beating her breast with her hands, lacerating herself, and disfigur-
ing her own face with the blood from his wounds, she called him
her lord, her husband, her emperor, and seemed to have pretty
nearly forgotten all her own evils, she was so intent upon his mis-
fortunes. Antony, stopping her lamentations as well as he could,
called for wine to drink, either that he was thirsty, or that he
imagined that it might put him the sooner out of pain. When he
had drunk, he advised her to bring her own affairs, so far as might
be honourably done, to a safe conclusion, and that, among all the
friends of Caesar, she should rely on Proculeius; that she should
not pity him in this last turn of fate, but rather rejoice for him in
remembrance of his past happiness, who had been of all men the
most illustrious and powerful, and in the end had fallen not ig-
nobly, a Roman by a Roman overcome.

Just as he breathed his last, Proculeius arrived from Caesar . . .
She, however, was careful not to put herself in Proculeius's
power; but from within her monument, he standing on the outside of a door, on the level of the ground, which was strongly
barred, but so that they might well enough hear one another's
voice, she held a conference with him; she demanding that her
kingdom might be given to her children, and he binding her to
be of good courage, and trust Caesar in everything.

Having taken particular notice of the place, he returned to Caesar, and Gallus was sent to parley with her the second time; who,
being come to the door, on purpose prolonged the conference,
while Proculeius fixed his scaling-ladders in the window through
which the women had pulled up Antony. And so entering, with
two men to follow him, he went straight down to the door where
Cleopatra was discoursing with Gallus. One of the two women
who were shut up in the monument with her cried out, "Miser-

and her eyes sunk in her head. The marks of the blows she had given herself were visible about her bosom, and altogether her whole person seemed no less afflicted than her soul. But, for all this, her old charm, and the boldness of her youthful beauty, had not wholly left her, and in spite of her present condition, still sparkled from within, and let itself appear in all the movements of her countenance. Caesar, desiring her to repose herself, sat down by her; and, on this opportunity, she said something to justify her actions, attributing what she had done to the necessity she was under, and to her fear of Antony; and when Caesar, on each point, made his objections, and she found herself confuted, she broke off at once into language of entreaty and deprecation, as if she desired nothing more than to prolong her life. And at last, having by her a list of her treasure, she gave it into his hands; and when Seleucus, one of her stewards, who was by, pointed out that various articles were omitted, and charged her with secreting them, she flew up and caught him by the hair, and struck him several blows on the face. Caesar smiling and withholding her, "Is it not very hard, Caesar," said she, "when you do me the honour to visit me in this condition I am in, that I should be accused by one of my own servants of laying by some women's toys, not meant to adorn, be sure, my unhappy self, but that I might have some little present by me to make your Octavia and your Livia, that by their intercession I might hope to find you in some measure disposed to mercy?" Caesar was pleased to hear her talk thus, being now assured that she was desirous to live. And, therefore, letting her know that the things she had laid by she might dispose of as she pleased, and his usage of her should be honourable above her expectation, he went away, well satisfied that he had overreached her, but, in fact, was himself deceived.

There was a young man of distinction among Caesar's companions named Cornelius Dolabella. He was not without a certain tenderness for Cleopatra, and sent her word privately, as she had besought him to do, that Caesar was about to return through Syria, and that she and her children would be sent on within three days. When she understood this, she made her request to Caesar that he would be pleased to permit her to make oblations to the departed Antony; which being granted, she ordered herself to be carried to the place where he was buried. . . .

Having made . . . lamentations, crowning the tomb with garlands and kissing it, she gave orders to prepare her a bath, and, coming out of the bath, she lay down and made a sumptuous meal. And a country fellow brought her a little basket, which the guards intercepting and asking what it was, the fellow put the leaves which lay uppermost aside, and showed them it was full of figs; and on their admiring the largeness and beauty of the figs, he laughed and invited them to take some, which they refused, and, suspecting nothing, bade him carry them in. After her repast, Cleopatra sent to Caesar a letter which she had written and sealed; and, putting everybody out of the monument but her two women, she shut the doors. Caesar, opening her letter, and finding pathetic prayers and entreaties that she might be buried in the same tomb with Antony, soon guessed what was doing. At first he was going himself in all haste, but, changing his mind, he sent others to see. The thing had been quickly done. The messengers came at full speed, and found the guards apprehensive of nothing; but on opening the door, they saw her stone-dead, lying upon a bed of gold, set out in all her royal ornaments. Iras, one of her women, lay dying at her feet, and Charmion, just ready to fall, scarce able to hold up her head, was adjusting her mistress's diadem. And when one that came in said angrily, "Was this well done of your lady, Charmion?" "Extremely well," she answered, "and as became the descendant of so many kings;" and as she said this, she fell down dead by the bedside.

E. Fuller (ed.), *Plutarch: Lives of Ten Noble Greeks and Romans* (New York, 1978): 597–605.

Notes

"A Queen Issued from So Many Kings"

1. See the contemporary papyri, such as *Ägyptische Urkunden aus den Staatlichen Museum zu Berlin, Griechische Urkunden* 8 (Berlin, 1895), nos. 1835, 1843, and passim (hereafter cited as *Berliner Griechische Urkunden*).

2. Plutarch, "Antony," 86.

3. *Geography* XVII, no. 1: 11.

4. J. Whitehorne, in *Akten des 21. internationalen Papyrologenkongresses in Berlin 1995* (Stuttgart, 1997): 1009–13; I do not share his conclusions.

5. F. Jacoby, *Die Fragmente der griechischen Historiker,* 3 vols. (Berlin, 1923–1958), no. 260, F 2.14.

6. Plutarch, "Antony," 27.

7. W. Huss, *Aegyptus* 70 (1990): 191–203.

8. See Cicero's lost *De Rege alexandrino* (On the king of Alexandria); idem, *De Lege agraria* (On the agrarian law) II: 17, 44.

9. W. Dittenberger, *Orientis Graeci inscriptiones selectae* 2 (Leipzig, 1905; reprint ed., Hildesheim, 1960): 741.

10. Cicero, *Epistulae ad familiares* (Letters to his family) VIII: 4.

11. H.W. Fairman in R. Mond and O.H. Myers, *The Bucheum* 2 (London, 1934): 11–13.

12. Valerius Maximus, *Factorum et dictorum memorabilium libri* (Collection of memorable deeds and words), IV: 1, 15.

13. E. Bernand, *Inscriptions grecques du Fayoum* 1 (Leiden, 1975), no. 205.

14. *Papiri greci e latini (PSI)* 10 (Florence, 1932), no. 1098.

15. Appian, *Civil War* II: 71. See also Plutarch, "Antony," 25, suggesting an improbable love affair between the younger Pompey and Cleopatra.

16. The conversion of pre-Julian dates of the Roman calendar follows G.

Radke, *Fasti Romani* (Münster, 1990). Another system, that of the astronomer U. Le Verrier, has been defended in particular by J. Carcopino, *Jules César* (Paris, 1935): 11–14.

17. *Berliner Griechische Urkunden* 8, no. 1730.

18. P. Cairo Dem. 30616 a and b.

19. See most recently M. Chauveau in *Akten des 21. internationalen Papyrologenkongresses in Berlin 1995,* 168–70.

20. T.C. Skeat, *Journal of Egyptian Archaeology* 48 (1962): 101. In the lacuna after the name of the queen, it is tempting to restore "[king Ptolemy]," that is, the name of her younger brother, whom Cleopatra might have associated with her revolt.

21. Caesar, *Bellum civile* (Civil war) III: 103, cited here in the translation by R. Warner, *War Commentaries of Caesar* (New York, 1960): 328.

22. A. Burnett et al., *Roman Provincial Coinage* 1 (London, 1992): 673–74, no. 4866.

23. "Pompey," 77–80.

24. Dio Cassius, *Roman History* XLII, 7, claims that Theodotos presented the head of Pompey to Caesar on his ship, before he could even disembark, but the time frame seems too brief to allow for such a possibility. Further, we scarcely see how Ptolemy's camp could have been warned of such a sudden arrival.

25. *Bellum civile;* Warner (trans.), *War Commentaries of Caesar:* 330.

26. See Chauveau, *Akten des 21. internationalen Papyrologenkongresses,* 168–70.

27. Appian, *Civil War* II: 90.

28. Suetonius, *Lives of the Twelve Caesars,* "Julius Caesar," 52: 3.

29. Julius Caesar, *Bellum alexandrinum* (Alexandrian war), 33.

The New Aphrodite

1. These triumphs celebrated the successive defeats of the Gauls, the Alexandrians, Pharnakes, and King Juba of Numidia, the latter an ally of the Pompeians in Africa. Caesar had to avoid any celebration of victories over Roman citizens in the civil war.

2. Dio Cassius, *Roman History* XLIII, 27: 3.

3. Cicero, *Ad Atticum* XIV, 8: 1; 20: 2; XV, 1: 5; 4: 4; 15: 2; 17: 2.

4. Suetonius, *Lives of the Twelve Caesars,* "Julius Caesar," 52: 3; Dio Cassius, *Roman History* XLIV, 7: 3.

5. Appian, *Civil War* II, 102; Dio Cassius, *Roman History* LI, 22: 3.

6. Pliny, *Natural History* XVIII, 25, 57, 211.

7. Suetonius, "Julius Caesar," 42.

8. See, for example, R. Étienne, *Jules César* (Paris, 1997), in which Cleopatra is dealt with in three pages (62–65) out of three hundred.

9. Suetonius, "Julius Caesar," 83.

10. *Ad Atticum* XIV, 8: 1.

11. The birth of the child, called Caesarion to distinguish him from Julius Caesar, is usually dated to June 23, 47, the date I myself adopted in *Egypt in the Age of Cleopatra* (Ithaca, 2000), 25. On the basis of new information that will be discussed in a future article, it now seems preferable, at least with regard to the date, to follow the hypothesis of J. Carcopino, *Passion et politique chez les Césars* (Paris, 1958): 34–37.

12. Cicero, *Ad Atticum* XIV, 20: 2.

13. Suetonius, "Julius Caesar," 52.

14. This question has been much debated; cf. T. Schrapel, *Das Reich der Kleopatra* (Trier, 1996): 106–9.

15. A. Burnett et al., *Roman Provincial Coinage* I (London, 1992): 578, no. 3901.

16. *Ad Atticum* XV, 15: 2, in which he is called by the diminutive "Sara."

17. *Antiquities of the Jews* XV, 89.

18. In particular, Cleopatra-Berenike in the year 80; she was constrained to marry her cousin Ptolemy XI, who quickly had her assassinated. There was also Berenike IV, who had several unfortunate betrothals before marrying Archelaos in 56.

19. By way of comparison, the Egypt annexed by Octavian would be occupied by an army consisting of only three legions, which were quickly reduced to two.

20. W. Peremans and E. Van't Dack, *Prosopographia Ptolemaica* I (Louvain, 1950) and 8 (Louvain, 1975), no. 33.

21. Ibid., no. 194.

22. A. Bernand, *La Prose sur pierre* (Paris, 1992), no. 46.

23. J. Bingen, *Chronique d'Égypte* 70 (1995): 206–22.

24. Appian, *Civil Wars* IV, 59.

25. Ibid., 61.

26. Ibid., 63.

27. Dio Cassius, *Roman History* XLVII, 31: 5.

28. Appian, *Civil Wars* IV, 74, 82; cf. V, 8.

29. Plutarch, "Antony," 3.

30. Ibid., 12.

31. Ibid., 24.

32. See Suetonius, "Julius Caesar," 44; Plutarch, "Caesar," 58: 2.

33. Plutarch, "Antony," 25.

34. Appian, *Civil Wars* V, 8.

35. "Antony," 25; E. Fuller (ed.), *Plutarch: Lives of Ten Noble Greeks and Romans* (New York, 1978): 541.

36. Ibid., 26.

37. Appian, *Civil Wars* V, 9; Josephus, *Antiquities* XV, 89; Dio Cassius, *Roman History* XLVIII, 24: 2.

38. Plutarch, "Life of Antony," 28.

39. W. Dittenberger, *Orientis Graeci Inscriptiones Selectae* I (Leipzig, 1903; reprint ed., Hildesheim, 1986): 195; inscription dated to December 28, 34. We do not follow the interpretation of P.M. Fraser, *Journal of Roman Studies* 47 (1957): 71–73.

40. "Antony," 29; Fuller (ed.), *Plutarch*, 546.

41. Plutarch, "Antony," 36.

42. Josephus, *Wars of the Jews* I, 279; *Antiquities* XIV, 375–76.

43. Joesephus, *Wars* I, 282–85.

44. Plutarch, "Antony," 33.

45. This was Archelaos, the husband of Berenike IV, who was killed when Ptolemy XII returned from exile in 55.

46. Schrapel, *Das Reich der Kleopatra*.

47. Porphyry of Tyre, in F. Jacoby, *Die Fragmente der griechischen Historiker*, no. 260, F 2.17.

48. Plutarch, "Antony," 37–51; Dio Cassius, *Roman History* XLIX, 22–33.

49. Plutarch, "Antony," 53.

50. Dio Cassius, *Roman History* XLIX, 38: 1.

51. Appian, *Civil Wars* V, 144.

52. Dio Cassius, *Roman History* XLIX, 39: 2.

53. Josephus, *Antiquities* XV, 96; *Wars* I, 362.

54. Dio Cassius, *Roman History* XLIX, 40: 2; 44: 2; Plutarch, "Antony," 53.

55. Dio Cassius, *Roman History* XLIX, 40: 3–4.

56. "Antony," 54.

57. *Roman History* XLIX, 41: 1–3.

58. M.H. Crawford, *Roman Republican Coinage* (London, 1974): 543/1.

59. Burnett et al., *Roman Provincial Coinage* I, nos. 4094–96: 601–2.

Cleopatra, Enemy of Rome

1. Dio Cassius, *Roman History* L, 1: 3–5; Plutarch, "Antony," 55.

2. Suetonius, "Augustus," 69.

3. Plutarch, "Antony," 56.

4. Ibid., 57.

5. Ibid., 58; Dio Cassius, *Roman History* L, 3, 5.

6. Plutarch, "Comparison of Demetrios and Antony," 3.

7. M.H. Crawford, *Roman Republican Coinage* (London, 1974): 544.

8. Plutarch, "Antony," 59.

9. Ibid., 56. Antony changed his mind just before the battle of Actium; see ibid., 63.

10. The kings are listed in Plutarch, "Antony," 61.

11. Dio Cassius, *Roman History* L, 15: 2.

12. Ibid., L, 5: 4.

13. Plutarch, "Antony," 66; Dio Cassius, *Roman History* L, 33: 1–3.

14. Plutarch, "Antony," 67.

15. Dio Cassius, *Roman History* LI, 5: 3–5.

16. Plutarch, "Antony," 69; Dio Cassius, *Roman History* LI, 6: 2–3.

17. Plutarch, "Antony," 71.

18. Dio Cassius, *Roman History* LI, 6: 5–6.

19. Ibid., LI, 8: 6–7; Plutarch, "Antony," 73.

20. Dio Cassius, *Roman History* LI, 9: 5–6; Plutarch, "Antony," 74, treating the rumor as dubious.

21. Dio Cassius, *Roman History* LI, 15: 5.

22. See T.C. Skeat, *Journal of Roman Studies* 43 (1953): 98–100.

23. "Antony," 76–86.

24. *Roman History* LI, 10–14.

25. "Antony," 84. This was surely a relative of the Dolabella who was vanquished by Cassius at Laodicea in 43.

26. Horace, *Odes* I, 37: 21.

27. *Libertatis P.R. Vindex;* see R. Syme, *The Roman Revolution* (Oxford, 1939): 306.

28. Strabo, *Geography* XVII, 1, 10.

29. "Antony," 86.

30. *Roman History* LI, 14: 1–2.

31. See M. Grant, *Cleopatra* (London, 1972): 227. For a good illustration of this iconography, see the exhibit catalogue by N. Grimal et al., *La Gloire d'Alexandrie* (Paris, 1998): 281, no. 222.

32. See, for example, J.G. Griffiths, *Journal of Egyptian Archaeology* 47 (1961): 113–18.

33. See Skeat, *Journal of Roman Studies* 43 (1953): 98–100.

34. Paulus Orosius, *Historiarum adversus paganos libri septem* VI, 19, 20.

35. Plutarch, "Antony," 80.

36. Dio Cassius, *Roman History* LI, 16: 5.

Conclusion: *The Memory of Cleopatra*

1. Plutarch, "Antony," 86.

2. Graffito Philae 370, 8; see F.L. Griffiths, *Catalogue of the Demotic Graffiti of the Dodecaschoenus* (Oxford, 1937): 104.

3. For a treatment of this topic, see L. Hughes-Hellet, *Cleopatra: Histories, Dreams and Distortions* (London, 1990).

4. See H.W. Fairman, in R. Mond and O.H. Myers, *The Bucheum* 2 (London, 1934): 11–13.

5. Thus, inter alia, M. Grant, *Cleopatra* (London, 1972): 99–100. The thesis has been refuted by J. Quaegebeur, *Göttinger Miszellen* 120 (1991): 52, no. 19.

6. *Ägyptische Urkunden aus den Staatlichen Museum zu Berlin, Griechische Urkunden* XIV (Berlin, 1980), no. 2376.

7. This epithet can also be viewed as a partial transposition of the title Pater Patriae ("father of his country") borne by Cicero and then by Caesar in 45; see R. Étienne, *Jules César* (Paris, 1997): 213.

8. See A. Farid, *Fünf demotische Stelen aus Berlin, Chicago, Durham, London und Oxford* (Berlin, 1995): 32–76. My reading of the first line is rather different from his.

Bibliography

Curious readers will first be interested in the ancient authors, among whom Plutarch is readily available in various English translations. Information also can be gleaned from Suetonius, *The Twelve Caesars,* translated by R. Graves and published in a paperback edition by Penguin. Appian, Dio Cassius, and Flavius Josephus are all to be found in the Loeb Classical Library. Book XVII of Strabo's *Geography,* invaluable for its description of Egypt written only a few year after the death of the queen, is also available in a translation by H.L. Jones in the Loeb Classical Library. Papyrological sources are scarcely available except to specialists.

On life in Egypt in the Ptolemaic era, see my *Egypt in the Age of Cleopatra* (Ithaca, 2000). On Alexandria, see N. Grimal et al., *La Gloire d'Alexandrie* (Paris, 1998), which is a catalogue of an exhibit on display at the Petit-Palais from May 7 to July 26, 1998. For the general context of the Hellenistic world, see P. Green, *Alexander to Actium: An Essay on the Historical Evolution of the Hellenistic Age,* Hellenistic Culture and Society 1 (Berkeley, 1990). For the Roman point of view, see the older but still excellent volume by R. Syme, *The Roman Revolution* (Oxford, 1939).

Modern biographies of Cleopatra are legion, but few warrant reading. For German readers, there is M. Klaus's excellent little *Kleopatra* (Munich, 1995). The important work by H. Volkmann,

Bibliography

Kleopatra: Politik und Propaganda, is available in an English translation by T.J. Cadoux, *Cleopatra: A Study in Politics and Propaganda* (London, 1958). The present work owes much to M. Grant, *Cleopatra* (London, 1972), which has had several editions; it can always be consulted with interest, despite a certain number of arguable errors of interpretation. Irène Frain's recent French work *L'Inimitable* (Paris, 1998) is practically a fiction, well documented but antihistorical in its lack of critical acumen and its excessive subjectivity.

Index

Index

Index